GO FOR
GOLD

GO FOR GOLD

Inspiration *to* Increase
Your Leadership Impact

JOHN C. MAXWELL

THOMAS NELSON
Since 1798

NASHVILLE DALLAS MEXICO CITY RIO DE JANEIRO BEIJING

Published in Nashville, Tennessee, by Thomas Nelson.
Thomas Nelson is a trademark of Thomas Nelson, Inc.

Published in association with Yates & Yates, LLP, www.yates2.com.

Thomas Nelson, Inc., titles may be purchased in bulk for educational, business, fund-raising, or sales promotional use. For information, please e-mail SpecialMarkets@ThomasNelson.com.

Adapted from *The Maxwell Daily Reader*

Library of Congress Cataloging-in-Publication Data

Maxwell, John C., 1947–
Go for gold : inspiration to increase your leadership impact / John C. Maxwell.
p. cm.
ISBN 978-1-4002-0225-6 (hardcover)
ISBN 978-1-4002-8037-7 (IE)
1. Leadership. I. Title.
HD57.7.M39425 2008
658.4'092—dc22   2008003381

Printed in the United States of America
08 09 10 11 QW 6 5 4 3

CONTENTS

A NOTE FROM JOHN C. MAXWELL

Dear Friend,

We live in a time of instant gratification. If we want to read a book or listen to music, we download it in a matter of minutes. If we're hungry, we order food and it arrives at our door. If we want to see a movie, we get it on demand for our home theater, and we microwave popcorn to eat while we watch it. Unfortunately, we expect the same kind of speed when it comes to personal growth. We want it to be just as quick and easy. It will never happen.

If you want to become a better leader, you need to give up a microwave mentality. Forget speed and become like a Crock-Pot. Personal growth takes time. It takes seasoning. And it requires heat. It's slow, but like something cooked in a Crock-Pot, it's worth waiting for!

We've developed *Go for Gold* as a companion to *Leadership Gold* to help you with the long, slow process of leadership development. Think of it as the seasoning that will help you develop depth as you marinate in leadership.

Divided into twenty-six weeks, this volume contains leadership instruction that complements *Leadership Gold* as you read and work through its application exercises. It will provide you with a bit of extra mentoring and encouragement, drawn from the best of my other books.

If you're a highly motivated (or impatient) person whose desire is to advance quickly, twenty-six weeks may seem like a long time. But remember, what's worth having is worth working for.

You cannot become a great leader overnight, but you can become a better leader day by day. I trust this resource will help you with the process.

Your friend,
John

WEEK 1

―――――― ∾ ――――――

IF IT'S LONELY AT THE TOP,
YOU'RE NOT DOING
SOMETHING RIGHT

KEY GROWTH QUESTIONS FOR THE WEEK

Are you better at the science or art of leadership?

Why do you want to be at the top?

How big is your dream?

TO LEADERSHIP, ADD FRIENDSHIP

Why do I recommend that you work to develop friendships on the job?

Friendship Is the Foundation of Influence: President Abraham Lincoln said, "If you would win a man to your cause, first convince him that you are his sincere friend." Good relationships make influence possible, and friendship is the most positive relationship you can develop on the job with your coworkers.

Friendship Is the Framework for Success: I believe long-term success is unachievable without good people skills. Theodore Roosevelt said, "The most important single ingredient in the formula of success is knowing how to get along with people." Without it, most achievements are not possible, and even what we do achieve can feel hollow.

Friendship Is the Shelter Against Sudden Storms: If you're having a bad day, who can make you feel better? A friend. When you have to face your fears, who would you rather do it with? A friend. When you fall on your face, who can help pick you up? A friend. Aristotle was right when he said, "True friends are a sure refuge."

—*The 360° Leader*

Don't just be a teammate—be a friend
to those you work with.

DO THINGS TOGETHER AS A TEAM

I once read the statement, "Even when you've played the game of your life, it's the feeling of teamwork that you'll remember. You'll forget the plays, the shots, and the scores, but you'll never forget your teammates." That is describing the community that develops among teammates who spend time doing things together.

The only way to develop community and cohesiveness among your teammates is to get them together, not just in a professional setting but in personal ones as well. There are lots of ways to get yourself connected with your teammates, and to connect them with one another. Many families who want to bond find that camping does the trick. Business colleagues can socialize outside work (in an appropriate way). The where and when are not as important as the fact that team members share common experiences.

—*The 17 Indisputable Laws of Teamwork*

Spend some time with your team and share an enjoyable common experience.

THOSE CLOSEST TO THE LEADER

In more than thirty years of leadership, I have learned that those closest to the leader will determine the success level of that leader. A negative reading of this statement is also true: Those closest to the leader will determine the level of failure for that leader. The positive or negative outcome in my leadership depends upon my ability to develop those closest to me.

Stop for a moment and think of the five or six people closest to you in your organization. Are you developing them? Do you have a game plan for them? Are they growing? Have they been able to lift your load?

In their first training session, I give new leaders this principle: *As a potential leader you are either an asset or a liability to the organization.* I illustrate this truth by saying, "When there's a problem, a 'fire' in the organization, you as a leader are often the first to arrive at the scene. You have in your hands two buckets. One contains water and the other contains gasoline. The 'spark' before you will either become a greater problem because you pour the gasoline on it, or it will be extinguished because you use the bucket of water."

The question a leader needs to ask is, "Am I training them to use the gasoline or the water?"

—*Developing the Leaders Around You*

Have you trained the people closest to you in your organization to be water carriers?

DEVELOP A PERSONAL RELATIONSHIP WITH THE PEOPLE YOU EQUIP

All good mentoring relationships begin with a personal relationship. As your people get to know and like you, their desire to follow your direction and learn from you will increase. If they don't like you, they will not want to learn from you, and the equipping process slows down or even stops.

To build relationships, begin by listening to people's life stories, their journeys so far. Your genuine interest in them will mean a lot to them. It will also help you to know their personal strengths and weaknesses. Ask them about their goals and what motivates them. Find out what kind of temperaments they have. You certainly don't want to equip and develop a person whose greatest love is numbers and financial statements for a position where he would be spending 80 percent of his time dealing with disgruntled customers.

One of the best ways to get to know people is to see them outside of the business world. People are usually on their guard at work. They try to be what others want them to be. By getting to know them in other settings, you can get to know who they really are. Try to learn as much as you can about the people and do your best to win their hearts. If you first find their hearts, they'll be glad to give you their hands.

—*Developing the Leaders Around You*

*Make an appointment to get to know someone
on your team today.*

VALUE AND REWARD LOYALTY

A quality you should look for in people to join you on your journey is loyalty. Although this alone does not ensure success in another person, a lack of loyalty is sure to ruin your relationship with him or her. Think of it this way: When you're looking for potential leaders, if someone you're considering lacks loyalty, he is disqualified. Don't even consider taking him on the journey with you because in the end, he'll hurt you more than help you. So what does it mean for others to be loyal to you?

They love you unconditionally. They accept you with your strengths and weaknesses intact. They genuinely care for you, not just for what you can do for them.

They represent you well to others. Loyal people always paint a positive picture of you with others. They may take you to task privately or hold you accountable, but they never criticize you to others.

They are able to laugh and cry with you as you travel together. Loyal people are willing and able to share your joys and sorrows. They make the trip less lonely.

They make your dream their dream. Some people will undoubtedly share the journey with you only briefly. You help one another for a while and then go your separate ways. But a few— a special few—will want to come alongside you and help you for the rest of the journey. These people make your dream their dream. If you find people like that, take good care of them.

—*Your Road Map for Success*

Do you inspire loyalty? Show gratitude to the loyal people in your inner circle today.

NOTES

_____
_____
_____
_____
_____
_____
_____
_____
_____
_____
_____
_____
_____
_____
_____
_____
_____
_____
_____
_____
_____
_____

WEEK 2

THE TOUGHEST PERSON TO LEAD IS ALWAYS YOURSELF

KEY GROWTH QUESTIONS FOR THE WEEK

How clearly do you see yourself?

Where do you need to grow?

How well do you take advice?

FEELINGS FOLLOW THINKING

The human mind has a tremendous amount of power in our lives. That which holds our attention determines our actions. Because of that, where we are today is the result of the dominating thoughts in our minds. And the way we think determines what our attitudes are. The good news is that you and I can change that. You can control your thoughts, and because of that, you can control your attitude.

Let's do an experiment that will show you what I mean. Take a moment to think about the place where you live. No problem. You decided to think about it, and you did it. Next, imagine for a moment that the place where you live has burned to the ground, and everything in it is gone. What kind of emotional response did you have? Maybe you were sad because many irreplaceable things would have been lost in a fire. Maybe you were happy because your current living situation is terrible and a fresh start would do you good. The point is that your thinking prompts your emotion. That's key, and here's why:

Major premise: We can control our thoughts.
Minor premise: Our feelings come from our thoughts.
Therefore: We can control our feelings by changing
how we think.

Why is that important? Because your attitude is your emotional approach to life. It's the framework through which you see events, other people, even yourself. That's why I believe the saying, "You are not what you think you are, but what you think . . . you are."

—*The Difference Maker*

*How are the dominating thoughts of your mind affecting
your attitude and effectiveness as a leader?*

THE POWER OF SELF-DISCIPLINE

Author H. Jackson Brown Jr. quipped, "Talent without discipline is like an octopus on roller skates. There's plenty of movement, but you never know if it's going to be forward, backwards, or sideways." If you know you have talent, and you've seen a lot of motion—but little concrete results—you may lack self-discipline.

Sort out your priorities. Think about which two or three areas of life are most important to you. Write them down, along with the disciplines that you must develop to keep growing and improving in those areas. Develop a plan to make the disciplines a daily or weekly part of your life.

List the reasons. Take the time to write out the benefits of practicing the disciplines you've just listed. Then post the benefits someplace where you will see them daily. On the days when you don't want to follow through, reread your list.

Get rid of excuses. Write down every reason why you might not be able to follow through with your disciplines. Read through them. You need to dismiss them as the excuses they are. Even if a reason seems legitimate, find a solution to overcome it. Don't leave yourself any reasons to quit. Remember, only in the moment of discipline do you have the power to achieve your dreams.

A nursery in Canada displays this sign on its wall: "The best time to plant a tree is twenty-five years ago . . . The second best time is today." Plant the tree of self-discipline in your life today.

—*The 21 Indispensable Qualities of a Leader*

Begin a routine of regularly scheduled actions of self-discipline.

MEASURING INTEGRITY

Take some time to answer these questions today:

1. How well do I treat people from whom I can gain nothing?
2. Am I transparent with others?
3. Do I role-play based on the person(s) I'm with?
4. Am I the same person when I'm in the spotlight as I am when I'm alone?
5. Do I quickly admit wrongdoing without being pressed to do so?
6. Do I put other people ahead of my personal agenda?
7. Do I have an unchanging standard for moral decisions, or do circumstances determine my choices?
8. Do I make difficult decisions, even when they have a personal cost attached to them?
9. When I have something to say about people, do I talk *to* them or *about* them

—*Becoming a Person of Influence*

**Come back to this statement throughout the day:
Leadership begins with integrity.**

TO IMPROVE YOUR LEADERSHIP,
IMPROVE YOURSELF

A danger of teaching conferences or writing books like this one is that people start to assume you're an expert who has mastered everything you teach. Don't believe it. Like you, I'm still working on my relational and leadership skills. There are principles that I don't do well, so I'm still working to improve myself. And that will always be true for me. If I ever think I've finished growing, then I'm in trouble.

People who often experience relational difficulties are tempted to look at everyone but themselves to explain the problem. But we must always begin by examining ourselves and being willing to change whatever deficiencies we have. Critic Samuel Johnson advised that "he who has so little knowledge of human nature as to seek happiness by changing anything but his own disposition will waste his life in fruitless efforts and multiply the grief which he purposes to remove."

—*Winning with People*

What must you change in yourself to become a better leader?

DISCIPLINED EMOTIONS

People have just two choices when it comes to their emotions: they can master their emotions or be mastered by them. That doesn't mean that to be a good team player, you have to turn off your feelings. But it does mean that you shouldn't let your feelings prevent you from doing what you should or drive you to do things you shouldn't.

A classic example of what can happen when a person doesn't discipline his emotions can be seen in the life of golf legend Bobby Jones. Like today's Tiger Woods, Jones was a golf prodigy. He began playing in 1907 at age five. By age twelve, he was scoring below par, an accomplishment most golfers don't achieve in a lifetime of playing the game. At age fourteen, he qualified for the U.S. Amateur Championship. But Jones didn't win that event. His problem can be best described by the nickname he acquired: "club thrower." Jones often lost his temper—and his ability to play well.

An older golfer whom Jones called Grandpa Bart advised the young man, "You'll never win until you can control that temper of yours." Jones took his advice and began working to discipline his emotions. At age twenty-one, Jones blossomed and went on to be one of the greatest golfers in history, retiring at age twenty-eight after winning the grand slam of golf. Grandpa Bart's comment sums up the situation: "Bobby was fourteen when he mastered the game of golf, but he was twenty-one when he mastered himself."

—*The 17 Essential Qualities of a Team Player*

Have you mastered your emotions,
or are you mastered by them?

NOTES

WEEK 3

❧

DEFINING MOMENTS DEFINE
YOUR LEADERSHIP

KEY GROWTH QUESTIONS FOR THE WEEK

What is your track record?

How are you managing your decisions?

How prepared are you for future defining moments?

SEEK A BREAKTHROUGH

Every major difficulty you face in life is a fork in the road. You choose which track you will head down, toward breakdown or breakthrough. Dick Biggs, a consultant who helps Fortune 500 companies improve profits and increase productivity, writes that all of us have unfair experiences; as a result, some people merely exist and adopt a "cease and desist" mentality. He continues,

> One of the best teachers of persistence is your life's critical turning points. Expect to experience 3–9 turning points or "significant changes" in your life. These transitions can be happy experiences . . . or unhappy times such as job losses, divorce, financial setbacks, health problems and the death of loved ones. Turning points can provide perspective, which is the ability to view major changes within the larger framework of your lifetime and let the healing power of time prevail. By learning from your turning points, you can grow at a deeper level within your career and life.

If you've been badly hurt, then start by acknowledging the pain and grieving any loss you may have experienced. Then forgive the people involved—including yourself, if needed. Doing that will help you move on. Just think, *today* may be your day to turn the hurts of your past into a breakthrough for the future.

—*Failing Forward*

Determine to turn difficult experiences
into breakthrough moments.

LET FAILURE POINT YOU TO SUCCESS

Oliver Goldsmith was born the son of a poor preacher in Ireland in the 1700s. Growing up, he wasn't a great student. In fact, his schoolmaster labeled him a "stupid blockhead." He did manage to earn a college degree, but he finished at the bottom of his class. He was unsure of what he wanted to do. At first he tried to become a preacher, but it didn't suit him, and he was never ordained. Next he tried law but failed at it. He then settled on medicine, but he was an indifferent doctor and was not passionate about his profession. He was able to hold several posts only temporarily. Goldsmith lived in poverty, was often ill, and once even had to pawn his clothes to buy food.

It looked like he would never find his way. But then he discovered an interest and aptitude for writing and translating. At first, he worked as a Fleet Street reviewer and writer. But then he began to write works that came out of his own interests. He secured his reputation as a novelist with *The Vicar of Wakefield*, a poet with "The Deserted Village," and a playwright with *She Stoops to Conquer*.

My friend Tim Masters says that failure is the productive part of success. It provides the road you don't have to travel again, the mountain you don't have to climb again, and the valley you don't have to cross again. At the time you're making mistakes, they may not feel like "the kiss of Jesus," which was Mother Teresa's term for failures that drive us to God. But if we have the right attitude, they can lead us to what we ought to be doing.

—*The Difference Maker*

Embrace your failures as blessings in disguise.

FOCUS ON THE BIG PICTURE

On an October evening in 1968, a group of die-hard spectators remained in Mexico City's Olympic Stadium to see the last finishers of the Olympic marathon. More than an hour before, Mamo Wolde of Ethiopia had won the race to the exuberant cheers of onlookers. But as the crowd watched and waited for the last participants, it was getting cool and dark.

It looked as if the last runners were finished, so the remaining spectators were breaking up and leaving when they heard the sounds of sirens and police whistles coming from the marathon gate into the stadium. And as everyone watched, one last runner made his way onto the track for the last lap of the twenty-six-mile race. It was John Stephen Akhwari from Tanzania. As he ran the 400-meter circuit, people could see that his leg was bandaged and bleeding. He had fallen and injured it during the race, but he hadn't let it stop him. The people in the stadium rose and applauded until he reached the finish line.

As he hobbled away, he was asked why he had not quit, injured as he was and having no chance of winning a medal. "My country did not send me to Mexico City to start the race," he answered. "They sent me to finish the race."

Akhwari looked beyond the pain of the moment and kept his eye on the big picture of why he was there. As you make the success journey, keep in mind that your goal is to finish the race—to do the best you're capable of doing.

—*Your Road Map for Success*

Be more than just a racer today. Be a finisher.

WILL YOU SPLATTER OR BOUNCE?

If only life could become easier with every day of living! But that's not reality, is it? As you get older, truly some things get harder, but others also get easier. In every stage of life, there are good aspects and bad. The key is to focus on the good and learn to live with the bad. Of course, not everyone does that. In fact, I've found that there are really only two kinds of people in this world when it comes to dealing with discouragement: splatters and bouncers. When splatters hit rock bottom, they fall apart, and they stick to the bottom like glue. On the other hand, when bouncers hit bottom, they pull together and bounce back.

Paul J. Meyer, founder of the Success Motivation Institute, says, "Ninety percent of those who fail are not actually defeated. They simply quit." That's what discouragement can do to you if you don't handle it the right way—it can cause you to quit. Since you *will* become discouraged at some point, the question is, *Are you going to give up or get up?*

—*The Difference Maker*

Make the decision to get up and bounce back today.

BECOMING MORE SOLUTION ORIENTED

How do you look at life? Do you see a solution in every challenge or a problem in every circumstance? To make yourself a more solution-oriented team player . . .

Refuse to give up. Think about an impossible situation you and your teammates have all but given up overcoming. Now determine to not give up until you find a solution.

Refocus your thinking. No problem can withstand the assault of sustained thinking. Set aside dedicated time with key teammates to work on the problem. Make sure it's prime think time, not leftover time when you're tired or distracted.

Rethink your strategy. Get out of the box of your typical thinking. Break a few rules. Brainstorm absurd ideas. Redefine the problem. Do whatever it takes to generate fresh ideas and approaches to the problem.

Repeat the process. If at first you don't succeed in solving the problem, keep at it. If you do solve the problem, then repeat the process with another problem. Remember, your goal is to cultivate a solution-oriented attitude that you bring into play all the time.

—*The 17 Essential Qualities of a Team Player*

Do you see a problem in every circumstance or
a solution in every challenge?

NOTES

_____

_____

_____

_____

_____

_____

_____

_____

_____

_____

_____

_____

_____

_____

_____

_____

_____

_____

_____

_____

_____

_____

WEEK 4

~~~~~

WHEN YOU GET KICKED IN THE REAR, YOU KNOW YOU'RE OUT IN FRONT

KEY GROWTH QUESTIONS FOR THE WEEK

How secure are you as a leader?

What are your deficiencies?

How can you properly process criticism?

FOLLOWING COLUMBUS

In the book *Principle Centered Leadership*, Stephen Covey tells how Columbus was once invited to a banquet where he was given the most honored place at the table. A shallow courtier who was jealous of him asked abruptly, "Had you not discovered the Indies, are there not other men in Spain who would have been capable of the enterprise?"

Columbus made no reply but took an egg and invited the company to make it stand on end. They all attempted to do it, but none succeeded, whereupon the explorer tapped it on the table, denting one end, and left it standing.

"We all could have done it that way!" the courtier cried.

"Yes, if you had only known how," answered Columbus. "And once I showed you the way to the New World, nothing was easier than to follow it."

The truth is that it's a hundred times easier to criticize others than to find solutions to problems. But criticism gets you nowhere.

Alfred Armand Montapert said, "The majority see the obstacles; the few see the objectives; history records the successes of the latter, while oblivion is the reward of the former."

—*Becoming a Person of Influence*

*Do not allow others' criticism to discourage you
from moving forward as a leader.*

SECURE LEADERS CAN TAKE THE HEAT

Insecure leaders are dangerous—to themselves, their followers, and the organizations they lead. That's because a leadership position becomes an amplifier of personal flaws. Whatever negative baggage you have in life only gets more difficult to bear when you're trying to lead others.

Insecure leaders have several common traits:

1. *They Don't Provide Security for Others:* There's an old saying: "You cannot give what you do not have."

2. *They Take More from People than They Give:* Insecure people are on a continual quest for validation, acknowledgment, and love. Because of that, their focus is on finding security, not instilling it in others. They are primarily takers rather than givers, and takers do not make good leaders.

3. *They Continually Limit Their Best People:* Show me an insecure leader, and I'll show you someone who cannot genuinely celebrate his people's victories. Insecure leaders hoard power. In fact, the better his people are, the more threatened he is.

4. *They Continually Limit Their Organization:* When followers are undermined and receive no recognition, they become discouraged and eventually stop performing at their potential. And when that happens, the entire organization suffers.

—*The 21 Indispensable Qualities of a Leader*

Are insecurities hindering your potential as you lead others?

THE HIGHER YOU GO,
THE GREATER THE PROBLEMS

A common misconception about successful people is that they achieve what they do because they don't have problems. But that simply isn't true. In his book *Holy Sweat*, Tim Hansel tells this story:

> In 1962, Victor and Mildred Goertzel published a revealing study of 413 famous and exceptionally gifted people. The study was called *Cradles of Eminence*. These two researchers spent years trying to understand the source of these people's greatness, the common thread which ran through all of these outstanding people's lives. The most outstanding fact was that almost all of them, 392, had to overcome very difficult obstacles in order to become who they were. Their problems became opportunities instead of obstacles.

Not only do people overcome obstacles to become successful, even after they have achieved a level of success, they continue to face problems. The bad news is that the higher a person goes— personally and professionally—the more complicated life gets. The good news is that if he continues to grow and develop himself, his ability to deal with those problems will also increase.

—*Becoming a Person of Influence*

Are you growing in such a way that you are better equipped to deal with your problems?

LEADERS CAN'T TAKE
REJECTION PERSONALLY

When your ideas are not received well by others, do your best to not take it personally. When someone in a meeting does that, it can kill the creative process, because at that point the discussion becomes about the person whose feelings are hurt. If you can stop competing and focus your energy on creating, you will open the way for the people around you to take their creativity to the next level.

If you don't have any personal experience in the publishing world, then I'm guessing that you believe authors always select the titles of their books. While that may be the way it works for some authors, it has not been the case for me. I've written more than forty books, yet I think I've selected the titles for about a dozen of them.

A book is a pretty personal thing for an author. Why would I allow someone else to pick the title? Because I know my ideas aren't always the best ideas. I often think they are, but when everyone in the room has a different opinion, it pays to listen. That's why I've adopted the attitude that the company owner doesn't need to win—the best idea does.

Be passionate about your work and have the integrity to stand up for your ideas. Without passion you will not be taken seriously. When principle is involved, don't budge. Most matters, though, involve taste or opinion, not principle. In these areas recognize that you can compromise. If you become someone who can never compromise, you will forfeit opportunities to those who can.

—*The 360° Leader*

Let the best ideas win to help the organization move forward.

TAKING THE HEAT

During the term of President Ronald Reagan, leaders of seven industrial nations were meeting at the White House to discuss economic policy. During the meeting Canadian prime minister Pierre Trudeau strongly upbraided British prime minister Margaret Thatcher, telling her that she was all wrong and that her policies wouldn't work. She stood there in front of him with her head up, listening until he was finished. Then she walked away.

Reagan went up to her and said, "Maggie, he should never have spoken to you like that. He was out of line, just entirely out of line. Why did you let him get away with that?"

Thatcher looked at Reagan and answered, "A woman must know when a man is being simply childish."

That story surely typifies Margaret Thatcher. She appeared to have no doubts about herself or her beliefs—and she was absolutely secure in her leadership as a result. That is the case for all great leaders.

Secure leaders are able to believe in others because they believe in themselves. They aren't arrogant; they know their own strengths and weaknesses and respect themselves. When their people perform well, they don't feel threatened. They go out of their way to bring the best people together and then build them up so that they will perform at the highest level. And when a secure leader's team succeeds, it brings him great joy. He sees that as the highest compliment he can receive.

—*The 21 Indispensable Qualities of a Leader*

Do you believe in yourself enough to graciously
take the heat as a leader?

NOTES

WEEK 5

∽

NEVER WORK A DAY
IN YOUR LIFE

KEY GROWTH QUESTIONS FOR THE WEEK

What is your true passion?

How much passion do you have for your current work?

How can you follow your passion?

PRIORITIZE YOUR LIFE ACCORDING TO YOUR PASSION

People who have passion but lack priorities are like individuals who find themselves in a lonely log cabin deep in the woods on a cold snowy night and then light a bunch of small candles and place them all around the room. They don't create enough light to help them see, nor do they produce enough heat to keep them warm. At best, they merely make the room seem a bit more cheerful. On the other hand, people who possess priorities but no passion are like those who stack wood in the fireplace of that same cold cabin but never light the fire. But people who have passion with priorities are like those who stack the wood, light the fire, and enjoy the light and heat that it produces.

In the early 1970s, I realized that my talent would be maximized and my potential realized only if I matched my passion with my priorities. I was spending too much of my time doing tasks for which I possessed neither talent nor passion. I had to make a change—to align what I felt strongly about with what I was doing. It made a huge difference in my life. It didn't eliminate my troubles or remove my obstacles, but it empowered me to face them with greater energy and enthusiasm. For more than thirty years, I have worked to maintain that alignment of priorities and passion. And as I have, I've kept in mind this quote by journalist Tim Redmond, which I put in a prominent place for a year to keep me on track: "There are many things that will catch my eye, but there are only a few that catch my heart. It is those I consider to pursue."

—*Talent Is Never Enough*

Make sure your passion and priorities are aligned today.

THE POWER OF A DREAM

I believe that each of us has a dream placed in the heart. I'm not talking about wanting to win the lottery. That kind of idea comes from a desire to escape our present circumstances, not to pursue a heartfelt dream. I'm talking about a vision deep inside that speaks to the very soul. It's the thing we were born to do. It draws on our talents and gifts. It appeals to our highest ideals. It sparks our feelings of destiny. It is inseparably linked to our purpose in life. The dream starts us on the success journey.

A dream does many things for us:

- A dream gives us direction
- A dream increases our potential
- A dream helps us prioritize
- A dream adds value to our work
- A dream predicts our future

Oliver Wendell Holmes noted, "The great thing in this world is not so much where we are but in what direction we are moving." This is also one of the great things about having a dream. You can pursue your dream no matter where you are today. And what happened in the past isn't as important as what lies ahead in the future. As the saying goes, "No matter what a person's past may have been, his future is spotless." You can begin pursuing your dream today!

—*Your Road Map for Success*

Dare to dream and act on that dream.

MAKE THE MOST OF YOUR GIFTS
AND OPPORTUNITIES

More than thirty years ago I memorized a quote that has shaped the way I live: "My potential is God's gift to me. What I do with my potential is my gift to Him." I believe I am accountable to God, others, and myself for every gift, talent, resource, and opportunity I have in life. If I give less than my best, then I am shirking my responsibility. I believe UCLA coach John Wooden was speaking to this idea when he said, "Make every day your masterpiece." If we give our very best all the time, we can make our lives into something special. And that will overflow into the lives of others.

There's a story I love about President Dwight Eisenhower. He once told the National Press Club that he regretted not having a better political background so that he would be a better orator. He said his lack of skill in that area reminded him of his boyhood days in Kansas when an old farmer had a cow for sale. The buyer asked the farmer about the cow's pedigree, butterfat production, and monthly production of milk. The farmer said, "I don't know what a pedigree is, and I don't have an idea about butterfat production, but she's a good cow, and she'll give you all the milk she has." That's all any of us can do—give all that we have. That's always enough.

—*25 Ways to Win with People*

Strive to make the most of your potential today.

HAVE YOU FOUND YOUR NICHE?

Have you found your niche? As you fulfill your responsibilities, do you find yourself thinking something like, *There's no place like this place anywhere near this place, so this must be the place*? If so, then stay the course and keep growing and learning in your area of expertise. If not, you need to get on track.

If you know what your niche is but aren't working in it, start planning a transition. It could be as simple as a change in duties or as complex as a change of career. No matter whether it will require six weeks or six years, you need a transition plan and a timetable for completing it. Once you're certain of your course, have the courage to take the first step.

If you have no idea what you should be doing, you need to do some research. Talk to your spouse and close friends about your strengths and weaknesses. Ask for your leader's assessment. Take personality or temperament tests. Look for recurring themes in your life. Try to articulate your life purpose. Do whatever it takes to find clues concerning where you should be. Then try new things related to your discoveries. The only way to find your niche is to gain experience.

—*The 17 Indisputable Laws of Teamwork*

If you haven't already, find your niche and continue growing within it.

INCREASING YOUR PASSION

I s passion a characteristic of your life? Do you wake up feeling enthusiastic about your day? Is the first day of the week your favorite, or do you live from weekend to weekend? How long has it been since you couldn't sleep because you were too excited by an idea? You can never lead something you don't care passionately about. You can't start a fire in your organization unless one is first burning in you. To increase your passion, do the following:

Take your temperature. How passionate are you about your life and work? Does it show? Get an honest assessment by querying several coworkers and your spouse about your level of desire.

Return to your first love. Think back to when you were just starting out in your career—or even farther back to when you were a child. What really turned your crank? What could you spend hours and hours doing? Try to recapture your old enthusiasm. Then evaluate your life and career in light of those old loves.

Associate with people of passion. It sounds hokey, but birds of a feather really do flock together. If you've lost your fire, get around some firelighters. Passion is contagious. Schedule some time with people who can infect you with it.

—*The 21 Indispensable Qualities of a Leader*

Spend some time with passionate people today.

NOTES

WEEK 6

◆◈◆

THE BEST LEADERS
ARE LISTENERS

KEY GROWTH QUESTIONS FOR THE WEEK

Give yourself a listening audit.

Who doesn't feel listened to?

What people have you neglected to seek out?

LISTEN WITH YOUR HEART

Herb Cohen, often called the world's best negotiator, says, "Effective listening requires more than hearing the words transmitted. It demands that you find meaning and understanding in what is being said. After all, meanings are not in words, but in people." Many people put their focus on the ideas being communicated, and they almost seem to forget about the person. You can't do that and listen with the heart.

There's a difference between listening passively and listening aggressively. To listen with your heart, your listening has to be active. In his book *It's Your Ship*, Captain Michael Abrashoff explains that people are more likely to speak aggressively than to listen aggressively. When he decided to become an intentional listener, it made a huge difference in him and his team.

—*25 Ways to Win with People*

Choose to be an aggressive listener today.

THE VALUE OF LISTENING

Edgar Watson Howe once joked, "No man would listen to you talk if he didn't know it was his turn next." Unfortunately, that accurately describes the way too many people approach communication—they're too busy waiting for their turn to really listen to others. But people of influence understand the incredible value of becoming a good listener. For example, when Lyndon B. Johnson was a junior senator from Texas, he kept a sign on his office wall that read, "You ain't learnin' nothin' when you're doing all the talkin'." And Woodrow Wilson, the twenty-eighth American president, once said, "The ear of the leader must ring with the voices of the people."

The ability to skillfully listen is one key to gaining influence with others. Consider these benefits to listening that we've found:

- Listening shows respect
- Listening builds relationships
- Listening increases knowledge
- Listening generates ideas
- Listening builds loyalty

Roger G. Imhoff urged, "Let others confide in you. It may not help you, but it surely will help them." At first glance, listening to others may appear to benefit only them. But when you become a good listener, you put yourself in a position to help yourself too. You have the ability to develop strong relationships, gather valuable information, and increase your understanding of yourself and others.

Focus on listening to others today.

THE VOICES OF VISION

Where does vision come from? To find the vision that is indispensable to leadership, you have to become a good listener. You must listen to several voices.

The Inner Voice: Vision starts within. Do you know your life's mission? What stirs your heart? What do you dream about? If what you're pursuing in life doesn't come from a desire within— from the very depths of who you are and what you believe—you will not be able to accomplish it.

The Unhappy Voice: Where does inspiration for great ideas come from? From noticing what doesn't work. Discontent with the status quo is a great catalyst for vision. Are you on complacent cruise control? Or do you find yourself itching to change your world? No great leader in history has fought to prevent change.

The Successful Voice: Nobody can accomplish great things alone. To fulfill a big vision, you need a good team. But you also need good advice from someone who is ahead of you in the leadership journey. If you want to lead others to greatness, find a mentor. Do you have an adviser who can help you sharpen your vision?

The Higher Voice: Although it's true that your vision must come from within, you shouldn't let it be confined by your limited capabilities. A truly valuable vision must have God in it. Only He knows your full capabilities. Have you looked beyond yourself, even beyond your own lifetime, as you've sought your vision? If not, you may be missing your true potential and life's best for you.

—*The 21 Indispensable Qualities of a Leader*

As a leader, are you listening not only to people but
also to these other important voices?

UNDERSTANDING PEOPLE
PAYS GREAT DIVIDENDS

The ability to understand people is one of the greatest assets anyone can ever have. It has the potential to positively impact every area of your life, not just the business arena. For example, look at how understanding people helped this mother of a preschooler. She said,

> Leaving my four-year-old son in the house, I ran out to throw something in the trash. When I tried to open the door to get back inside, it was locked. I knew that insisting that my son open the door would have resulted in an hour-long battle of the wills. So in a sad voice, I said, "Oh, too bad. You just locked yourself in the house." The door opened at once.

Understanding people certainly impacts your ability to communicate with others. David Burns, a medical professor of psychiatry at the University of Pennsylvania, observed, "The biggest mistake you can make in trying to talk convincingly is to put your highest priority on expressing your ideas and feelings. What most people really want is to be listened to, respected, and understood. The moment people see that they are being understood, they become more motivated to understand your point of view." If you can learn to understand people—how they think, what they feel, what inspires them, how they're likely to act and react in a given situation—then you can motivate and influence them in a positive way.

—*Becoming a Person of Influence*

Make understanding people your top priority today.

BE IMPRESSED, NOT IMPRESSIVE

Too often we think that if we can impress others, we will gain influence with them. We want to become others' heroes—to be larger than life. That creates a problem because we're real live human beings. People can see us for who we really are. If we make it our goal to impress them, we puff up our pride and end up being pretentious—and that turns people off.

If you want to influence others, don't try to impress them. Pride is really nothing more than a form of selfishness, and pretense is only a way to keep people at arm's length so that they can't see who you really are. Instead of impressing others, let them impress you.

It's really a matter of attitude. The people with charisma, those who attract others to themselves, are individuals who focus on others, not themselves. They ask questions of others. They listen. They don't try to be the center of attention. And they never try to pretend they're perfect.

—*The 360° Leader*

Listen with the purpose of understanding today, and benefit from the knowledge, experience, and perspective of others.

NOTES

WEEK 7

~∞~

GET IN THE ZONE
AND STAY THERE

KEY GROWTH QUESTIONS FOR THE WEEK

Have you identified your strength zone?

Is your job utilizing your strengths?

Are you leading team members into their strength zones?

DEVELOP THE TALENT YOU HAVE, NOT THE ONE YOU WANT

One thing I teach people at my conferences is to stop working on their weaknesses and start working on their strengths. (By this I mean abilities, not attitude or character issues, which *must* be addressed.) It has been my observation that people can increase their ability in an area by only 2 points on a scale of 1 to 10. For example, if your natural talent in an area is a 4, with hard work you may rise to a 6. In other words, you can go from a little below average to a little above average. But let's say you find a place where you are a 7; you have the potential to become a 9, maybe even a 10, if it's your greatest area of strength and you work exceptionally hard! That helps you advance from 1 in 10,000 talent to 1 in 100,000 talent—but only if you do the other things needed to maximize your talent.

—*Talent Is Never Enough*

Find your strengths and continually develop them.

ENCOURAGE THE DREAMS OF OTHERS

I consider it a great privilege when people share their dreams with me. It shows a great deal of courage and trust. And at that moment, I'm conscious that I have great power in their lives. That's no small matter. A wrong word can crush a person's dream; the right word can inspire him or her to pursue it.

If someone thinks enough of you to tell you about his or her dreams, take care. Actress Candice Bergen commented, "Dreams are, by definition, cursed with short life spans." I suspect she said that because there are people who don't like to see others pursuing their dreams. It reminds them of how far they are from living their own dreams. As a result, they try to knock down anyone who is shooting for the stars. By talking others out of their dreams, critical people excuse themselves for staying in their comfort zones.

Never allow yourself to become a dream killer. Instead, become a dream releaser. Even if you think another person's dream is far-fetched, that's no excuse for criticizing them.

—*25 Ways to Win with People*

Ask someone on your team to share their dream with you today.

PRACTICE YOUR CRAFT TODAY

William Osler, the physician who wrote *The Principles and Practice of Medicine* in 1892, once told a group of medical students:

> Banish the future. Live only for the hour and its allotted work. Think not of the amount to be accomplished, the difficulties to be overcome, or the end to be attained, but set earnestly at the little task at your elbow, letting that be sufficient for the day; for surely our plain duty is, as Carlyle says, "Not to see what lies dimly at a distance, but to do what lies clearly at hand."

The only way to improve is to practice your craft until you know it inside and out. At first, you do what you know to do. The more you practice your craft, the more you know. But as you do more, you will also discover more about what you ought to do differently. At that point you have a decision to make: Will you do what you have always done, or will you try to do more of what you think you should do? The only way you improve is to get out of your comfort zone and try new things.

People often ask me, "How can I grow my business?" or, "How can I make my department better?" The answer is for you personally to grow. The only way to grow your organization is to grow the leaders who run it. By making yourself better, you make others better. Retired General Electric CEO Jack Welch said, "Before you are a leader, success is all about growing yourself. When you become a leader, success is all about growing others." And the time to start is today.

—The 360° Leader

Focus your energy on trying something within your strength zone but outside of your comfort zone.

MAKE CHOICES THAT WILL
ADD VALUE TO TALENT

What creates the effectiveness necessary for converting talent into results? It comes from the choices you make. Orator, attorney, and political leader William Jennings Bryan said, "Destiny is not a matter of chance, it is a matter of choice; it is not a thing to be waited for, it is a thing to be achieved." I've discovered thirteen key choices that can be made to maximize any person's talent:

1. Belief lifts your talent.
2. Passion energizes your talent.
3. Initiative activates your talent.
4. Focus directs your talent.
5. Preparation positions your talent.
6. Practice sharpens your talent.
7. Perseverance sustains your talent.
8. Courage tests your talent.
9. Teachability expands your talent.
10. Character protects your talent.
11. Relationships influence your talent.
12. Responsibility strengthens your talent.
13. Teamwork multiplies your talent.

Make these choices, and you can become a talent-plus person. If you have talent, you stand alone. If you have talent *plus*, you stand out.
—*Talent Is Never Enough*

***Begin working on adding one of the above
qualities to your talent today.***

FIND A PURPOSE

More than anything else, having a sense of purpose keeps a person going in the midst of adversity. Business consultant Paul Stoltz did an extensive study on what it takes for individuals to persist through setbacks.

According to Stoltz, the most important ingredient of persistence is, "Identifying your mountain, your purpose in life, so that the work you do is meaningful. I run into people every day who are basically climbing the wrong mountain. People who have spent 20 years or more of their lives doing something that has no deep purpose for them. Suddenly they look back and go, 'What have I been doing?'"

If you are a purpose-driven person naturally, then you probably already possess an innate sense of direction that helps you overcome adversity. But if you're not, then you may need some help. Use the following steps to help you *develop a desire*.

- Get next to people who possess great desire.
- Develop discontent with the status quo.
- Search for a goal that excites you.
- Put your most vital possessions into that goal.
- Visualize yourself enjoying the rewards of that goal.

If you follow this strategy, you may not immediately find your ultimate purpose, but you will at least start moving in that direction. As Abraham Lincoln said, "Always bear in mind that your resolution to succeed is more important than any other thing."

—*Failing Forward*

How sure are you that you are climbing the right mountain?

NOTES

WEEK 8

—⁂—

A LEADER'S FIRST
RESPONSIBILITY IS TO
DEFINE REALITY

KEY GROWTH QUESTIONS FOR THE WEEK

What kind of thinker are you?

Who speaks truth in your life?

Where do you need a reality check?

CASTING VISION

If you are the leader of your team, then you carry the responsibility for communicating the team's vision and keeping it before the people continually. That's not necessarily easy. Whenever I endeavor to cast vision with the members of my team, I use the following checklist. I try to make sure that every vision message possesses . . .

- Clarity: brings understanding to the vision (answers what the people must know and what I want them to do)
- Connectedness: brings the past, present, and future together
- Purpose: brings direction to the vision
- Goals: bring targets to the vision
- Honesty: brings integrity to the vision and credibility to the vision caster
- Stories: bring relationships to the vision
- Challenge: brings stretching to the vision
- Passion: brings fuel to the vision
- Modeling: brings accountability to the vision
- Strategy: brings process to the vision

I believe your team members will find the vision more accessible and will more readily buy into it if you follow this checklist. And if they do, you will see that they have greater direction and confidence.

—The 17 Indisputable Laws of Teamwork

Recommunicate the vision to your people today.

TAKING A LOOK IN THE MIRROR

A few years ago when I traveled to New Zealand to do a confer-ence, I stayed in a hotel in Christchurch. One evening I was thirsty and started looking for a Coke machine. When I couldn't find one and I saw a door marked "Staff," I figured I'd go in and see if anyone in there could help me. I didn't find a hotel worker or a drink machine there, but I did observe something interesting. As I approached the door to go back out into the hall, I found that the door had a full-length mirror with the following words: "Take a good look at yourself. This is what the customer sees." The hotel's management was reminding employees that to fulfill their purpose, they needed to take a look at themselves.

And that's true for us too. Psychotherapist Sheldon Kopp believes "all the significant battles are waged within the self." As we examine ourselves, we discover what those battles are. And then we have two choices. The first is to be like the man who visited his doctor and found out he had serious health issues. When the doc-tor showed him his X-rays and suggested a painful and expensive surgery, the man asked, "Okay, but how much would you charge to just touch up the X-rays?"

The second choice is to stop blaming others, look at ourselves, and do the hard work of resolving the issues that are causing us problems. If you want to have better relationships with others, then stop, look in the mirror, and start working on yourself.

—*Winning with People*

The first reality you need to define is an accurate picture of yourself and your leadership ability.

BE MISSION-CONSCIOUS

Do you and your teammates keep the big picture in mind? Or do you tend to get so bogged down in the details of your responsibilities that you lose sight of the big picture? If you in any way hinder the bigger team—your organization—because of your desire to achieve personal success or even the success of your department, then you may need to take steps to improve your ability to keep the team's mission in mind.

Check to see if your team focuses on its mission. Start by measuring the clarity of the mission. Does your team or organization have a mission statement? If not, work to get the team to create one. If it does, then examine whether the goals of the team match its mission. If the values, mission, goals, and practices of a team don't match up, you're going to have a tough time as a team player.

Find ways to keep the mission in mind. If you're a strong achiever, the type of person who is used to working alone, or you tend to focus on the immediate rather than the big picture, you may need extra help being reminded of the mission of the team. Write down the mission and place it somewhere you can see it. Keep it in front of you so that you are always conscious of the team's mission.

Contribute your best as a team member. Once you're sure of the team's mission and direction, determine to contribute your best in the context of the team, not as an individual. That may mean taking a behind-the-scenes role for a while. Or it may mean focusing your inner circle in a way that contributes more to the organization, even if it gives you and your people less recognition.
—*The 17 Essential Qualities of a Team Player*

Avoid getting bogged down in details and keep the big picture in mind today.

DEFINING PROBLEMS

Philosopher Abraham Kaplan makes a distinction between problems and predicaments. A problem is something you can do something about. If you can't do something about it, then it's a predicament, something that must be coped with, endured.

When people treat a predicament as a problem, they can become frustrated, angry, or depressed. And when people treat problems as predicaments, they often settle, give up, or see themselves as victims.

More than twenty-five years ago I wrote something to help me see problems in the right light:

Predictors—helping to mold our future
Reminders—showing us that we cannot succeed alone
Opportunities—pulling us out of ruts, prompting creative thinking
Blessings—opening doors we would otherwise not go through
Lessons—providing instruction with each new challenge
Everywhere—telling us that no one is excluded from difficulties
Messages—warning us about potential disaster
Solvable—reminding us that every problem has a solution

If you can separate the predicaments from the problems, then you put yourself in a much better position to deal with the predicaments and to solve the problems.

—*The Difference Maker*

*Separate your predicaments from your problems today,
and deal with them accordingly.*

CHARTING THE COURSE

Nearly anyone can steer the ship, but it takes a leader to chart the course. Before leaders take their people on a journey, they become navigators and go through a process in order to give the trip the best chance of being a success:

Navigators Draw on Past Experience: Most natural leaders are activists. They tend to look forward—not backward—make decisions, and move on. But for leaders to become good navigators, they need to take time to reflect and learn from their experiences.

Navigators Examine the Conditions Before Making Commitments: Good navigators count the cost *before* making commitments for themselves and others. They examine not only measurable factors such as finances, resources, and talent, but also intangibles such as timing, morale, momentum, culture, and so on.

Navigators Listen to What Others Have to Say: No matter how good a leader you are, you yourself will not have all the answers. That's why top-notch navigators gather information from many sources.

Navigators Make Sure Their Conclusions Represent Both Faith and Fact: Being able to navigate for others requires a leader to possess a positive attitude. You've got to have faith that you can take your people all the way. On the other hand, you also have to be able to see the facts realistically. If you don't go in with your eyes wide open, you're going to get blindsided.

—*The 21 Irrefutable Laws of Leadership*

Have you taken the time to chart the course
for the people you're leading?

NOTES

WEEK 9

TO SEE HOW THE LEADER IS DOING, LOOK AT THE PEOPLE

Are your people following you?

How do you keep score?

Do you believe in your people?

PUT THE TEAM FIRST

Great developers of leaders think of the welfare of the team before thinking of themselves. Bill Russell was a gifted basketball player. Many consider him to be one of the best team players in the history of professional basketball. Russell observed, "The most important measure of how good a game I played was how much better I'd made my teammates play." That's the attitude necessary to become a great reproducer of leaders. The team has to come first.

Do you consider yourself to be a team player? Answer each of the following questions to see where you stand when it comes to promoting the good of the team:

1. Do I add value to others?
2. Do I add value to the organization?
3. Am I quick to give away the credit when things go right?
4. Is our team consistently adding new members?
5. Do I use my "bench" players as much as I could?
6. Do many people on the team consistently make important decisions?
7. Is our team's emphasis on creating victories more than producing stars?

—Becoming a Person of Influence

Develop a lifestyle of empowering others
and developing leaders.

LEADERSHIP IS EMPOWERMENT

How do you spot a leader? According to Robert Townsend, they come in all sizes, ages, shapes, and conditions. Some are poor administrators, while some are not overly bright. There is a clue: since some people are mediocre, the true leader can be recognized because somehow his people consistently demonstrate superior performances.

A leader is great, not because of his or her power, but because of his or her ability to empower others. Success without a successor is failure. A worker's main responsibility is developing others to do the work.

Loyalty to the leader reaches its highest peak when the follower has personally grown through the mentorship of the leader. Why? You win people's hearts by helping them grow personally.

Years ago, one of the key players on my staff was Sheryl Fleisher. When she first joined the team, she was not a people person. I began to work closely with her until she truly became a people person. Today she successfully develops others. There is a bond of loyalty that Sheryl has given to my leadership, and we both know the reason. My time invested with her brought a positive change. She will never forget what I have done for her. Interestingly, her time invested in the lives of others greatly helped me. I will never forget what she has done for me either.

The core of leaders who surround you should all be people you have personally touched or helped to develop in some way. When that happens, love and loyalty will be exhibited by those closest to you and by those who are touched by your key leaders.
—*Developing the Leader Within You*

*Are people going to the next level because
of your investment in them?*

ENLARGING OTHERS

Team members always love and admire a player who is able to help them go to another level, someone who enlarges them and empowers them to be successful.

Players who enlarge their teammates have several things in common:

1. Enlargers Value Their Teammates: Your teammates can tell whether you believe in them. People's performances usually reflect the expectations of those they respect.

2. Enlargers Value What Their Teammates Value: Players who enlarge others listen to discover what their teammates talk about and watch to see what they spend their money on. That kind of knowledge, along with a desire to relate to their fellow players, creates a strong connection.

3. Enlargers Add Value to Their Teammates: Adding value is really the essence of enlarging others. It's finding ways to help others improve their abilities and attitudes. An enlarger looks for the gifts, talents, and uniqueness in other people, and then helps them to increase those abilities.

4. Enlargers Make Themselves More Valuable: Enlargers work to make themselves better, not only because it benefits them personally, but also because it helps them to help others. If you want to increase the ability of a teammate, make yourself better.

How do your teammates see you? Are you an enlarger? Do you make them better than they are alone through your inspiration and contribution? Do you know what your teammates value? Do you capitalize on those things by adding value to them in those areas?

—*The 17 Essential Qualities of a Team Player*

Becoming a better leader starts with enlarging others regardless of whether or not you have position, authority, or a title.

FAITH IN OTHERS

His car drove past the unpainted barn and stopped in a cloud of summer dust at our front gate. I ran barefooted across the splintery porch and saw my uncle Henry bound out of the car. He was tall, very handsome, and terribly alive with energy. After many years overseas as a missionary in China, he was visiting our Iowa farm. He ran up to the old gate and put both of his big hands on my four-year-old shoulders. He smiled widely, ruffled my uncombed hair, and said, "Well! I guess you're Robert! I think you are going to be a preacher someday." That night I prayed secretly, "And dear God, make me a preacher when I grow up!" I believe that God made me a POSSIBILITY THINKER then and there.

—*Becoming a Person of Influence*

Help someone who doubts to have faith in himself today.

PEOPLE DO WHAT PEOPLE SEE

According to noted medical missionary Albert Schweitzer, "Example is not the main thing in influencing others . . . it is the only thing." Part of creating an appealing climate to grow potential leaders is modeling leadership. People emulate what they see modeled. Positive model—positive response. Negative model—negative response. What leaders do, potential leaders around them do. What they value, their people value. The leaders' goals become their goals. Leaders set the tone. As Lee Iacocca suggests, "The speed of the boss is the speed of the team." A leader cannot demand of others what he does not demand of himself.

As you and I grow and improve as leaders, so will those we lead. We need to remember that when people follow us, they can only go as far as we go. If our growth stops, our ability to lead will stop along with it. Neither personality nor methodology can substitute for personal growth. We cannot model what we do not possess. Begin learning and growing today, and watch those around you begin to grow. As a leader, I am primarily a follower of great principles and other great leaders.

—*Developing the Leaders Around You*

Ask no more of others than you are asking of yourself.

NOTES

WEEK 10

❧

DON'T SEND YOUR DUCKS
TO EAGLE SCHOOL

KEY GROWTH QUESTIONS FOR THE WEEK

Who have you put in the wrong place?

Do you need to free some eagles to soar and ducks to swim?

Do you know what potential leaders look like?

PUT PEOPLE IN THEIR (RIGHT) PLACE

Moving someone from a job they hate to the right job can be life changing. One executive I interviewed said he moved a person on his staff to four different places in the organization, trying to find the right fit. Because he'd placed her wrong so many times, he was almost ready to give up on her. But he knew she had great potential, and she was right for the organization. Finally, after he found the right job for her, she was a star!

Because this executive knows how important it is to have every person working in the right job, he asks his staff once a year, "If you could be doing anything, what would it be?" From their answers, he gets clues about any people who may have been miscast in their roles.

Trying to get the right person in the right job can take a lot of time and energy. Let's face it. Isn't it easier for a leader to just put people where it is most convenient and get on with the work? Once again, this is an area where leaders' desire for action works against them. Fight against your natural tendency to make a decision and move on. Don't be afraid to move people around if they're not shining the way you think they could.

—*The 360° Leader*

Look for clues that someone on your team could be better placed.

PEOPLE WITH LEADERSHIP POTENTIAL DON'T NEED A TITLE TO LEAD

If I had to identify the number one misconception people have about leadership, it would be the belief that leadership comes simply from having a position or title. But nothing could be further from the truth. You don't need to possess a position at the top of your group, department, division, or organization in order to lead. If you think you do, then you have bought into the position myth.

A place at the top will not automatically make anyone a leader. The Law of Influence in *The 21 Irrefutable Laws of Leadership* states it clearly: "The true measure of leadership is influence—nothing more, nothing less."

Because I have led volunteer organizations most of my life, I have watched many people become tied up by the position myth. When people who buy into this myth are identified as potential leaders and put on a team, they are very uncomfortable if they have not been given some kind of title or position that labels them as leaders in the eyes of other team members. Instead of working to build relationships with others on the team and to gain influence naturally, they wait for the positional leader to invest them with authority and give them a title. After a while, they become more and more unhappy, until they finally decide to try another team, another leader, or another organization.

People who follow this pattern don't understand how effective leadership develops.

—*The 360° Leader*

*If people need a title to lead, don't expect
them to soar like eagles.*

IDENTIFYING POTENTIAL LEADERS

There is something much more important and scarce than ability: it is the ability to recognize ability. One of the primary responsibilities of a successful leader is to identify potential leaders. It's not always an easy job, but it is critical.

Dale Carnegie was a master at identifying potential leaders. Once asked by a reporter how he had managed to hire forty-three millionaires, Carnegie responded that the men had not been millionaires when they started working for him. They had become millionaires as a result. The reporter next wanted to know how he had developed these men to become such valuable leaders. Carnegie replied, "Men are developed the same way gold is mined. Several tons of dirt must be moved to get an ounce of gold. But you don't go into the mine looking for dirt," he added. "You go in looking for the gold." That's exactly the way to develop positive, successful people. Look for the gold, not the dirt; the good, not the bad. The more positive qualities you look for, the more you are going to find.

—*Developing the Leaders Around You*

*Have you made it a priority to find potential
leaders and develop them?*

HOW TO SPOT AN EAGLE

Here is a list of twenty-five characteristics to help you rate and identify a potential leader.

0=Never   1=Seldom   2=Sometimes   3=Usually   4=Always

1. The person has influence. 0 1 2 3 4
2. The person has self-discipline. 0 1 2 3 4
3. The person has a good track record. 0 1 2 3 4
4. The person has strong people skills. 0 1 2 3 4
5. The person has the ability to solve problems. 0 1 2 3 4
6. The person does not accept the status quo. 0 1 2 3 4
7. The person sees the big picture. 0 1 2 3 4
8. The person has the ability to handle stress. 0 1 2 3 4
9. The person displays a positive spirit. 0 1 2 3 4
10. The person understands people. 0 1 2 3 4
11. The person is free of personal problems. 0 1 2 3 4
12. The person is willing to take responsibility. 0 1 2 3 4
13. The person is free from anger. 0 1 2 3 4
14. The person is willing to make changes. 0 1 2 3 4
15. The person has integrity. 0 1 2 3 4
16. The person is growing closer to God. 0 1 2 3 4
17. The person has the ability to see what must be done next. 0 1 2 3 4
18. The person is accepted as a leader by others. 0 1 2 3 4
19. The person has the ability and desire to keep learning. 0 1 2 3 4
20. The person has a manner that draws people. 0 1 2 3 4
21. The person has a good self-image. 0 1 2 3 4
22. The person has a willingness to serve others. 0 1 2 3 4

23. The person has the ability to bounce   0 1 2 3 4
    from problems.
24. The person has the ability to develop   0 1 2 3 4
    other leaders.
25. The person takes initiative.   0 1 2 3 4

Total Points:_____

Grading scale:
   90–100 Great leader (should be mentoring other good and
           great leaders)
    80–89 Good leader (must keep growing and keep mentoring
           others)
    70–79 Emerging leader (focus on growth)
    60–69 May have potential to lead (enter discovery process)
Below 60 Not currently a candidate for leadership development
                     —*Developing the Leaders Around You*

Evaluate the potential of leadership candidates
before investing in them.

PUT PEOPLE IN THEIR STRENGTH ZONES

In *The 17 Indisputable Laws of Teamwork*, the Law of the Niche says, "All players have a place where they add the most value." When leaders really get this, the teams they lead perform at an incredible level. And it reflects positively on those leaders. I don't think it is an exaggeration to say that the success of a leader is determined more by putting people into their strength zones than by anything else.

When I was in high school, I was fortunate to have a coach who understood this. During one of our varsity basketball practices, our coach, Don Neff, decided he wanted to teach us a very important lesson about basketball. He got the first- and second-string teams out on the floor to scrimmage. That wasn't unusual—we scrimmaged all the time. Our second team had some good players, but clearly the first team was much better. This time he had us do something very different from the norm. He let the second-string players take their normal positions, but he assigned each of us starters to a different role from our usual one. I was normally a shooting guard, but for this scrimmage I was asked to play center. And as I recall, our center was put in the point-guard position.

We were instructed to play to twenty, but the game didn't take long. The second team trounced us in no time. When the scrimmage was over, Coach Neff called us over to the bench and said, "Having the best players on the floor isn't enough. You have to have the best players in the right positions."

I never forgot that lesson. It doesn't matter what kind of a team you're leading. If you don't place people in their strength zones, you're making it almost impossible for them—and you—to win.

—*The 360° Leader*

Make sure your team members are in their strength zones.

NOTES

WEEK 11

KEEP YOUR MIND ON
THE MAIN THING

KEY GROWTH QUESTIONS FOR THE WEEK

What kinds of things occupy your time?

Are you focused on strengths?

Are you stuck in the middle?

PLANNED NEGLECT

William James said that the art of being wise is the "art of knowing what to overlook." The petty and the mundane steal much of our time. Too many of us are living for the wrong things.

Dr. Anthony Campolo tells about a sociological study in which fifty people over the age of ninety-five were asked one question: "If you could live your life over again, what would you do differently?" It was an open-ended question, and a multiplicity of answers constantly reemerged and dominated the results of the study. These were their answers:

- If I had it to do over again, I would reflect more.
- If I had it to do over again, I would risk more.
- If I had it to do over again, I would do more things that would live on after I am dead.

A young concert violinist was asked the secret of her success. She replied, "Planned neglect." Then she explained, "When I was in school, there were many things that demanded my time. When I went to my room after breakfast, I made my bed, straightened the room, dusted the floor, and did whatever else came to my attention. Then I hurried to my violin practice. I found I wasn't progressing as I thought I should, so I reversed things. Until my practice period was completed, I deliberately neglected everything else. That program of planned neglect, I believe, accounts for my success."

—*Developing the Leader Within You*

Put first things first today and neglect things
that don't really matter.

GOALS GIVE YOU "GO"

Millionaire industrialist Andrew Carnegie said, "You cannot push anyone up the ladder unless he is willing to climb himself." The same is true of a person on the success journey: she won't go forward unless she is motivated to do so. Goals can help provide that motivation. Paul Myer commented, "No one ever accomplishes anything of consequence without a goal. . . . Goal setting is the strongest human force for self-motivation."

Think about it. What is one of the greatest motivators in the world? Success. When you take a large activity (such as your dream) and break it down into smaller, more manageable parts (goals), you set yourself up for success because you make what you want to accomplish obtainable. And each time you accomplish a small goal, you experience success. That's motivating! Accomplish enough of the small goals, and you'll be taking a major step toward achieving your purpose and developing your potential.

Goals not only help you develop initial motivation by making your dreams obtainable, but they also help you continue to be motivated—and that creates momentum. Once you get going on the success journey, it will be very hard to stop you. The process is similar to what happens with a train. Getting it started is the toughest part of its trip. While standing still, a train can be prevented from moving forward by one-inch blocks of wood under each of the locomotive's drive wheels. However, once a train gets up to speed, not even a steel-reinforced concrete wall five feet thick can stop it.

—*Your Road Map for Success*

**Develop goals that will initiate motivation
and create momentum.**

THE VALUE OF TIME

Time is valuable. Psychiatrist and author M. Scott Peck said, "Until you value yourself, you won't value your time. Until you value your time, you will not do anything with it."

In *What to Do Between Birth and Death*, Charles Spezzano says that people don't pay for things with money; they pay for them with time. If you say to yourself, *In five years, I'll have put enough away to buy that vacation house*, then what you are really saying is that the house will cost you five years—one-twelfth of your adult life. "The phrase *spending your time* is not a metaphor," said Spezzano. "It's how life works."

Instead of thinking about what you do and what you buy in terms of money, instead think about them in terms of time. Think about it. What is worth spending your life on? Seeing your work in that light just may change the way you manage your time.

Action Step: List the top three things that consume your time every day. Are they worth spending your life on? If not, consider making some big changes.

—*The 360° Leader*

Are the tasks on today's agenda worthy of your life?

DEVELOPING COMPETENCY

A competent person does what he does well, continually persevering and distilling what's best—and he stops doing what he doesn't do well. Does that describe you? Do you focus your energy on what you can do well so that you become highly competent at it? Can your teammates depend on you to deliver in such a way that it brings the entire team success? If not, you may need to get better focused and develop the skills you need so that you can do your job and do it well.

To improve your competence . . .

Focus yourself professionally. It's hard to develop competence if you're trying to do everything. Pick an area in which to specialize. What is the one thing that brings together your skills, interests, and opportunities? Whatever it is, seize it.

Sweat the small stuff. Too many people don't take their work as far as they can. To do that, you need to develop an ability to get all the details right. That doesn't mean becoming a micromanager or control freak. It means doing the last 10 percent of whatever job you're doing. Try doing that on the next project or big task that is your responsibility.

Give more attention to implementation. Since implementation is often the most difficult part of any job, give it greater attention. How can you improve the gap between coming up with ideas and putting them into practice? Get your teammates together and discuss how you can improve the process.

—*The 17 Essential Qualities of a Team Player*

Be confident and competent with the details
so you're free to see the big picture.

LEADERS ARE INTENTIONAL

What does it mean to be intentional? It means working with purpose—making every action count. It's about focusing on doing the right things, moment to moment, day to day, and then following through with them in a consistent way.

Successful individuals are intentional. They aren't scattered or haphazard. They know what they're doing and why they're doing it. For a team to be successful, it needs intentional people who are able to remain focused and productive, people who make every action count.

How intentional are you? As you proceed through your day, do you have a plan and a purpose for everything you do? Do you know where you're going and why you're doing what you're doing? Or are you simply drifting down the stream of life? If your teammates don't detect a sense of intentionality in you, they won't know what to expect from you, and they will be unlikely to count on you when it really counts.

—*The 17 Essential Qualities of a Team Player*

Be intentional today. Make every action count.

NOTES

WEEK 12

❧

YOUR BIGGEST MISTAKE
IS NOT ASKING WHAT
MISTAKE YOU'RE MAKING

KEY GROWTH QUESTIONS FOR THE WEEK

What is your attitude toward mistakes?

Are you owning up to your mistakes?

Are you getting the best ideas from your subordinates?

WHEN FAILURE GETS YOU BY THE HEART

Let's face it. Failure can be very painful—sometimes physically and more often emotionally. Seeing part of your vision fall flat really hurts. And if people heap ridicule on top of your hurt feelings, you feel even worse. *The first important step in weathering failure is learning to not personalize it—making sure you know that your failure does not make you a failure.* But there's more to it than that. For many people the pain of failure leads to fear of failure. And they become like the person who says, "I'm too old to cry, but it hurts too much to laugh." That's when many people get stuck in the fear cycle. And if fear overcomes you, it's almost impossible to fail forward.

Playwright George Bernard Shaw asserted, "A life spent in making mistakes is not only more honorable but more useful than a life spent doing nothing." To overcome fear and break the cycle, you have to be willing to recognize that you will spend much of your life making mistakes. The bad news is that if you've been inactive for a long time, getting started is hard to do. The good news is that as soon as you start moving, it gets easier.

If you can take action and keep making mistakes, you gain experience. (That's why President Theodore Roosevelt said, "He who makes no mistakes makes no progress.") That experience eventually brings competence, and you make fewer mistakes. As a result, your fear becomes less paralyzing. But the whole cycle-breaking process starts with action. You must act your way into feeling, not wait for positive emotions to carry you forward.

—*Failing Forward*

What questions are you asking to make your mistakes opportunities for growth?

THE POWER OF FAILURE

Success doesn't mean avoiding failure. All of us fail. As we travel, we all hit potholes, take wrong turns, or forget to check the radiator. The only person who avoids failure altogether is the person who never leaves her driveway. So the real issue is not whether you're going to fail. It's whether you're going to fail successfully (profiting from your failure). As Nelson Boswell observed, "The difference between greatness and mediocrity is often how an individual views mistakes." If you want to continue on the success journey, you need to learn to fail forward.

Unsuccessful people are often so afraid of failure and rejection that they spend their whole lives avoiding risks or decisions that could lead to failure. They don't realize that success is based on their ability to fail and continue trying. When you have the right attitude, failure is neither fatal nor final. In fact, it can be a springboard to success. Leadership expert Warren Bennis interviewed seventy of the nation's top performers in various fields and found that none of them viewed their mistakes as failures. When talking about them, they referred to their "learning experiences," "tuition paid," "detours," and "opportunities for growth."

Successful people don't let failure go to their heads. Instead of dwelling on the negative consequences of failure, thinking of what might have been and how things haven't worked out, they focus on the rewards of success: learning from their mistakes and thinking about how they can improve themselves and their situations.

—*Your Road Map For Success*

Try to see failure as a learning experience today.

KEEP MISTAKES IN PERSPECTIVE

To leave the road of continual failure, a person must first utter the three most difficult words to say: "I was wrong." He has to open his eyes, admit his mistakes, and accept complete responsibility for his current wrong actions and attitudes. Every failure you experience is a fork in the road. It's an opportunity to take the right action, learn from your mistakes, and begin again.

Leadership expert Peter Drucker says, "The better a man is, the more mistakes he will make, for the more new things he will try. I would never promote to a top-level job a man who was not making mistakes . . . otherwise he is sure to be mediocre." Mistakes really do pave the road to achievement.

Here is an acronym I created to help me keep mistakes in perspective. Mistakes are . . .

Messages that give us feedback about life.
Interruptions that should cause us to reflect and think.
Signposts that direct us to the right path.
Tests that push us toward greater maturity.
Awakenings that keep us in the game mentally.
Keys that we can use to unlock the next door of opportunity.
Explorations that let us journey where we've never been before.
Statements about our development and progress.

—*Failing Forward*

Look for ways to praise your people's mistakes and help them learn from them today.

FAILING BACKWARD VERSUS
FAILING FORWARD

Look at the way any achiever approaches negative experiences, and you can learn a lot about how to fail forward. Read through these two lists, and determine which one describes your approach to failure:

Failing Backward	Failing Forward
Blaming Others	Taking Responsibility
Repeating Mistakes	Learning from Each Mistake
Expecting Never to Fail Again	Knowing Failure Is a Part of Progress
Expecting to Continually Fail	Maintaining a Positive Attitude
Accepting Tradition Blindly	Challenging Outdated Assumptions
Being Limited by Past Mistakes	Taking New Risks
Quitting	Persevering

Think about a recent setback you experienced. How did you respond? No matter how difficult your problems were, the key to overcoming them is in changing yourself. That in itself is a process, and it begins with a desire to be teachable. From this moment on, make a commitment to do whatever it takes to fail forward.

—*Failing Forward*

Maintain a teachable attitude in everything you do today.

CREATE AN ENVIRONMENT WHERE QUESTIONING IS SAFE

Pulitzer prize-winning historian Garry Wills said, "Followers have a say in what they are being led to. A leader who neglects that soon finds himself without followers." It takes secure leaders at the top to let the leaders working for them be full participants in the organization's leadership process. If leaders in the middle question them, they don't take it personally. When they share ideas, the top leaders cannot afford to feel threatened. When people lower than they are in the organization want to take risks, they need to be willing to give them room to succeed or fail.

Leadership by its very nature challenges. It challenges out-of-date ideas. It challenges old ways of doing things. It challenges the status quo. Never forget that what gets rewarded gets done. If you reward complacency, you will get complacency from your leaders in the middle. But if you can remain secure and let them find new ways of doing things—ways that are better than yours—the organization will move forward more quickly.

Instead of trying to be Mr. Answerman or Ms. Fix-it, when your leaders start coming into their own, move more into the background. Try taking on the role of wise counselor and chief encourager. Welcome the desire of your best leaders to innovate and improve the organization. After all, I think you'll agree that a win for the organization is a win for you.

So what role are you playing in your organization? Are you "the expert," or are you more of an advisor and advocate? Ask yourself, *Am I providing an environment where people can ask questions, share ideas, and take risks?*

—*The 360° Leader*

Encourage the people you lead to ask more questions.

NOTES

WEEK 13

Don't Manage Your Time—
Manage Your Life

Key Growth Questions for the Week

Are you squandering your time?

Are you getting help where you need it?

How do you decide how to spend your time?

MANAGE YOUR ENERGY

Some people have to ration their energy so that they don't run out. Up until a few years ago, that wasn't me. When people asked me how I got so much done, my answer was always, "High energy, low IQ." From the time I was a kid, I was always on the go.

Now I do have to pay attention to my energy level. In *Thinking for a Change*, I shared one of my strategies for managing my energy. When I look at my calendar every morning, I ask myself, *What is the main event?* That is the one thing to which I cannot afford to give anything less than my best. That one thing can be for my family, my employees, a friend, my publisher, the sponsor of a speaking engagement, or my writing time. I always make sure I have the energy to do it with focus and excellence.

Even people with high energy can have that energy sucked right out of them under difficult circumstances. Leaders in the middle of an organization often have to deal with what I call "the ABCs energy-drain."

Activity Without Direction—doing things that don't seem to matter
Burden Without Action—not being able to do things that really matter
Conflict Without Resolution—not being able to deal with what's the matter

If you find that you are in an organization where you often must deal with these ABCs, then you will have to work extra hard to manage your energy well. Either that or you need to look for a new place to work.

—*The 360° Leader*

Examine the ABCs. Where do you need to manage your energy?

FIGHT FOR INTEGRITY

Integrity is not what we do so much as who we are. And who we are, in turn, determines what we do. Our system of values is so much a part of us we cannot separate it from ourselves. It becomes the navigating system that guides us. It establishes priorities in our lives and judges what we will accept or reject.

We are all faced with conflicting desires. No one, no matter how "spiritual," can avoid this battle. Integrity is the factor that determines which desire will prevail. We struggle daily with situations that demand decisions between what we want to do and what we ought to do. Integrity establishes the ground rules for resolving these tensions. It determines who we are and how we will respond before the conflict even appears. Integrity welds what we say, think, and do into a whole person so that permission is never granted for one of those to be out of sync.

Integrity binds our person together and fosters a spirit of contentment within us. It will not allow our lips to violate our hearts. When integrity is the referee, we will be consistent; our beliefs will be mirrored by our conduct. There will be no discrepancy between what we appear to be and what our family knows we are, whether in times of prosperity or adversity.

Integrity is not only the referee between conflicting desires. It is the pivotal point between a happy person and a divided spirit. It frees us to be whole persons no matter what comes our way.

—*Developing the Leader Within You*

*Allow your integrity to be the referee in your
personal decision-making process.*

DECIDE WHAT YOU'RE NOT WILLING TO CHANGE

I have to admit that I'm a personal growth fanatic. There are few things I enjoy more than learning something new. My father got me started when I was a kid. He actually paid me to read books that would help me learn and grow. Now I'm over sixty, and I still love it when I can see myself improving in an area I've targeted for growth. But as much as I am dedicated to progress, there are some things that I'm not willing to change—no matter what—such as my faith and my values. I'd rather die than forfeit my faith in God or my commitment to integrity, family, generosity, and belief in people. Some things are not worth compromising at any price.

I want to encourage you to think about the nonnegotiables in your life. What are you willing to live and die for? Once you identify those things, then *everything* else should be open to change.

—*The Difference Maker*

What are the nonnegotiables in your life?

THE PARETO PRINCIPLE

Twenty percent of your priorities will give you 80 percent of your production, IF you spend your time, energy, money, and personnel on the top 20 percent of your priorities.

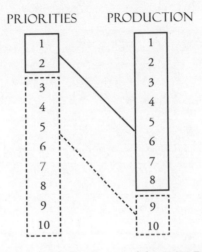

PRIORITIES PRODUCTION

The solid lines on the illustration of the 20/80 Principle above represent a person or organization that spends time, energy, money, and personnel on the most important priorities. The result is a four-fold return in productivity. The dotted lines represent a person or organization that spends time, energy, money, and personnel on the lesser priorities. The result is a very small return.

Examples of the Pareto Principle:

Time   20 percent of our time produces 80 percent
           of the results.
Counseling 20 percent of the people take up 80 percent
           of our time.

Products	20 percent of the products bring in 80 percent of the profit.
Reading	20 percent of the book contains 80 percent of the content.
Job	20 percent of our work gives us 80 percent of our satisfaction.
Speech	20 percent of the presentation produces 80 percent of the impact.
Donations	20 percent of the people will give 80 percent of the money.
Leadership	20 percent of the people will make 80 percent of the decisions.
Picnic	20 percent of the people will eat 80 percent of the food!

—*Leadership 101*

Are you expending 80 percent of your effort on the top 20 percent of your priorities?

MANAGE YOUR PERSONAL LIFE

You can do everything right at work and manage yourself well there, but if your personal life is a mess, it will eventually turn everything else sour. What would it profit a leader to climb to the top of the organizational chart but to lose a marriage or alienate the children? As someone who spent many years counseling people, I can tell you, no career success is worth it.

For years one of my definitions of *success* has been this: having those closest to me love and respect me the most. That is what is most important. I want the love and respect of my wife, my children, and my grandchildren before I want the respect of anyone I work with. Don't get me wrong. I want the people who work with me to respect me too, but not at the expense of my family. If I blow managing myself at home, then the negative impact will spill over into every area of my life, including work.

If you want to lead up, you must always lead yourself first. If you can't, you have no credibility. I've found the following to be true:

- If I can't lead myself, others won't follow me.
- If I can't lead myself, others won't respect me.
- If I can't lead myself, others won't partner with me.

That applies whether the influence you desire to exert is on the people above you, beside you, or below you. The better you are at making sure you're doing what you should be doing, the better chance you have for making an impact on others.

—*The 360° Leader*

How well are you leading yourself at home?

NOTES

WEEK 14

KEEP LEARNING TO
KEEP LEADING

KEY GROWTH QUESTIONS FOR THE WEEK

Do you have destination disease?

What is your plan?

Are you creating a growth environment?

ASK YOURSELF, AM I REALLY TEACHABLE?

All the good advice in the world won't help if you don't have a teachable spirit.

To know whether you are *really* open to new ideas and new ways of doing things, answer the following questions:

1. Am I open to other people's ideas?
2. Do I listen more than I talk?
3. Am I open to changing my opinion based on new information?
4. Do I readily admit when I am wrong?
5. Do I observe before acting on a situation?
6. Do I ask questions?
7. Am I willing to ask a question that will expose my ignorance?
8. Am I open to doing things in a way I haven't done before?
9. Am I willing to ask for directions?
10. Do I act defensive when criticized, or do I listen openly for the truth?

If you answered no to one or more of these questions, then you have room to grow in the area of teachability. Remember the words of John Wooden: "Everything we know we learned from someone else!"

—*Talent Is Never Enough*

*Soften your attitude, learn humility,
and remain teachable today.*

IT'S A MIND-SET

Teachability is an attitude, a mind-set that says, "No matter how much I know (or think I know), I can learn from this situation." That kind of thinking can help you turn adversity into advantage. It can make you a winner even during the most difficult circumstances. Sydney Harris sums up the elements of a teachable mind-set: "A winner knows how much he still has to learn, even when he is considered an expert by others. A loser wants to be considered an expert by others before he has learned enough to know how little he knows."

Business author Jim Zabloski writes,

Contrary to popular belief, I consider failure a necessity in business. If you're not failing at least five times a day, you're probably not doing enough. The more you do, the more you fail. The more you fail, the more you learn. The more you learn, the better you get. The operative word here is *learn*. If you repeat the same mistake two or three times, you are not learning from it. You must learn from your own mistakes and from the mistakes of others before you.

The ability to learn from mistakes has value not just in business, but in all aspects of life. If you live to learn, then you will really learn to live.

—*Failing Forward*

Do you think you have "arrived," or do you
maintain an attitude of teachability?

ARE YOU ADAPTABLE?

Teamwork and personal rigidity just don't mix. If you want to work well with others and be a good team player, you have to be willing to adapt yourself to your team. Team players who exhibit adaptability have certain characteristics. Adaptable people are . . .

Teachable: Diana Nyad said, "I am willing to put myself through anything; temporary pain or discomfort means nothing to me as long as I can see that the experience will take me to a new level. I am interested in the unknown, and the only path to the unknown is through breaking barriers." Adaptable people always place a high priority on breaking new ground. They are highly teachable.

Emotionally Secure: People who are not emotionally secure see almost everything as a challenge or a threat. They meet with rigidity or suspicion the addition of another talented person to the team, an alteration in their position or title, or a change in the way things are done. But secure people aren't made nervous by change itself. They evaluate a new situation or a change in their responsibilities based on its merit.

Creative: When difficult times come, creative people find a way. Creativity fosters adaptability.

Service Minded: People who are focused on themselves are less likely to make changes for the team than people focused on serving others. If your goal is to serve the team, adapting to accomplish that goal isn't difficult.

The first key to being a team player is being willing to adapt yourself to the team—not an expectation that the team will adapt to you!

—*The 17 Essential Qualities of a Team Player*

Are you willing to adapt to your team in order to succeed?

LEARN FLEXIBILITY

Perhaps the most relentless enemy of achievement, personal growth, and success is inflexibility. A friend sent me "The Top Ten Strategies for Dealing with a Dead Horse," which I think is hilarious:

1. Buy a stronger whip.
2. Change riders.
3. Appoint a committee to study the horse.
4. Appoint a team to revive the horse.
5. Send out a memo declaring the horse isn't really dead.
6. Hire an expensive consultant to find "the real problem."
7. Harness several dead horses together for increased speed and efficiency.
8. Rewrite the standard definition of *live horse*.
9. Declare the horse to be better, faster, and cheaper when dead.
10. Promote the dead horse to a supervisory position.

I bet you've seen just about every one of these "solutions" enacted in your place of work. But there's really only one effective way to deal with that problem: when your horse is dead, for goodness' sake, dismount. You don't have to love change to be successful, but you need to be willing to accept it.

—*Failing Forward*

*Look for a "dead horse" problem in your organization
and deal with it appropriately.*

YOU SET THE TONE

Leaders face the danger of contentment with the status quo. After all, if a leader already possesses influence and has achieved a level of respect, why should he keep growing? The answer is simple:

- Your growth determines who you are.
- Who you are determines who you attract.
- Who you attract determines the success of your organization.

If you want to grow your organization, you have to remain teachable. When I was a kid growing up in rural Ohio, I saw this sign in a feed store: "If you don't like the crop you are reaping, check the seed you are sowing." Though the sign was an ad for seeds, it contained a wonderful principle.

What kind of crop are you reaping? Do your life and leadership seem to be getting better day after day, month after month, year after year? Or are you constantly fighting just to hold your ground? If you're not where you hoped you would be by this time in your life, your problem may be lack of teachability. When was the last time you did something for the first time? When was the last time you made yourself vulnerable by diving into something for which you weren't the expert?

—The 21 Indispensable Qualities of a Leader

If you're not attracting the leaders you desire, spend more time developing yourself.

NOTES

_____

_____

_____

_____

_____

_____

_____

_____

_____

_____

_____

_____

_____

_____

_____

_____

_____

_____

_____

_____

WEEK 15

❧

LEADERS DISTINGUISH THEMSELVES DURING TOUGH TIMES

KEY GROWTH QUESTIONS FOR THE WEEK

Have you made the tough calls in the past?

Are you prepared to win the battle within?

Are you playing it too safe as a leader?

DON'T TRY TO AVOID PROBLEMS

There is a world of difference between a person who has a big problem and a person who makes a problem big. For several years I would do between twenty and thirty hours of counseling each week. I soon discovered that the people who came to see me were not necessarily the ones who had the most problems. They were the ones who were problem conscious and found their difficulties stressful. Naïve at first, I would try to fix their problems, only to discover that they would go out and find others.

A study of three hundred highly successful people, people like Franklin Delano Roosevelt, Helen Keller, Winston Churchill, Albert Schweitzer, Mahatma Gandhi, and Albert Einstein, reveals that one-fourth had handicaps, such as blindness, deafness, or crippled limbs. Three-fourths had either been born in poverty, come from broken homes, or at least come from exceedingly tense or disturbed situations.

Why did the achievers overcome problems, while thousands are overwhelmed by theirs? They refused to hold on to the common excuses for failure. They turned their stumbling blocks into stepping-stones. They realized they could not determine every circumstance in life, but they could determine their choice of attitude toward every circumstance.

The *Los Angeles Times* recently ran this quote: "If you can smile whenever anything goes wrong, you are either a nitwit or a repairman." I would add: or a leader in the making—one who realizes that the only problem you have is the one you allow to be a problem because of your wrong reaction to it. Problems can stop you temporarily. You are the only one who can do it permanently.

—*Developing the Leader Within You*

Learn to view your problems as temporary stumbling blocks.

ADVERSITY PROMPTS INNOVATION

Early in the twentieth century, a boy whose family had immigrated from Sweden to Illinois sent twenty-five cents to a publisher for a book on photography. What he received instead was a book on ventriloquism. What did he do? He adapted and learned ventriloquism. The boy was Edgar Bergen, and for more than forty years he entertained audiences with the help of a wooden dummy named Charlie McCarthy.

The ability to innovate is at the heart of creativity—a vital component in success. University of Houston professor Jack Matson recognized that fact and developed a course that his students came to call "Failure 101." In it, Matson assigns students to build mock-ups of products that no one would ever buy. His goal is to get students to equate failure with innovation instead of defeat. That way they will free themselves to try new things. "They learn to reload and get ready to shoot again," says Matson. If you want to succeed, you have to learn to make adjustments to the way you do things and try again.

—*Failing Forward*

What "problem" or "defeat" have you been dealt,
and how can you turn it into an asset?

ADVERSITY MOTIVATES

Nothing can motivate a person like adversity. Olympic diver Pat McCormick discusses this point: "I think failure is one of the great motivators. After my narrow loss in the 1948 trials, I knew how really good I could be. It was the defeat that focused all my concentration on my training and goals." McCormick went on to win two gold medals in the Olympics in Helsinki in 1952 and another two in Melbourne four years later.

If you can step back from the negative circumstances facing you, you will be able to discover their positive benefits. That is almost always true; you simply have to be willing to look for them—and not take the adversity you are experiencing too personally.

If you lose your job, think about the resilience you're developing. If you try something daring and survive, evaluate what you learned about yourself—and how it will help you take on new challenges. If a bookstore gets your order wrong, figure out whether it's an opportunity to learn a new skill. And if you experience a train wreck in your career, think of the maturity it's developing in you. Besides, Bill Vaughan maintains that "in the game of life it's a good idea to have a few early losses, which relieves you of the pressure of trying to maintain an undefeated season." Always measure an obstacle next to the size of the dream you're pursuing. It's all in how you look at it.

—Failing Forward

Embrace the adversities you may be facing in your life and retrain yourself to view them as beneficial.

BOUNCING BACK

About twenty years ago, *Time* magazine described a study by a psychologist of people who had lost their jobs three times due to plant closings. The writers were amazed by what they discovered. They expected the people being laid off to be beaten down and discouraged. Instead they found them to be incredibly resilient. Why was that? They concluded that people who had weathered repeated adversity had learned to bounce back. People who had lost a job and found a new one twice before were much better prepared to deal with adversity than someone who had always worked at the same place and had never faced adversity.

It may sound ironic, but if you have experienced a lot of failure, you are actually in a better position to achieve success than people who haven't. When you fail, and fail, and fail again—and keep getting back up on your feet and keep learning from your failures—you are building strength, tenacity, experience, and wisdom. And people who develop such qualities are capable of sustaining their success, unlike many for whom good things come early and easily. As long as you don't give up, you're in a really good place.

—*The Difference Maker*

It may sound ironic, but if you've failed a lot, celebrate.

RISE UP IN LEADERSHIP BY
SOLVING PROBLEMS

According to F. F. Fournies, writing in *Coaching for Improved Work Performance*, there are four common reasons why people do not perform the way they should:

1. They do not know *what* they are supposed to do.
2. They do not know *how* to do it.
3. They do not know *why* they should.
4. There are obstacles beyond their control.

These four reasons why people fail to perform at their potential are all the responsibilities of leadership. The first three reasons deal with starting a job correctly. A training program, job description, proper tools, and vision, along with good communication skills, will go a long way in effectively meeting the first three issues.

The fourth reason causes many people to fail to reach their performance potential. Problems continually occur at work, at home, and in life in general. My observation is that people don't like problems, weary of them quickly, and will do almost anything to get away from them. This climate makes others place the reins of leadership into your hands—*if* you are willing and able to either tackle their problems or train them to solve them. Your problem-solving skills will always be needed because people always have problems.

—*Developing the Leader Within You*

Look for problems you can help solve to help others and your organization.

NOTES

WEEK 16

～

PEOPLE QUIT PEOPLE,
NOT COMPANIES

KEY GROWTH QUESTIONS FOR THE WEEK

Can your people rely on you?

What is your attitude toward your people?

Do you express your appreciation?

OTHERS-FIRST THINKING

When you meet people, is your first thought about what they'll think of you or how you can make them feel more comfortable? At work, do you try to make your coworkers or employees look good, or are you more concerned about making sure that you receive your share of the credit? When you interact with family members, whose best interests do you have in mind? Your answers show where your heart is. To add value to others, you need to start putting others ahead of yourself in your mind and heart. If you can do it there, you will be able to put them first in your actions.

But how can anyone add value to others if he doesn't know what they care about? Listen to people. Ask them what matters to them. And observe them. If you can discover how people spend their time and money, you'll know what they value.

Once you know what matters to them, do your best to meet their needs with excellence and generosity. Offer your best with no thought toward what you might receive in return. President Calvin Coolidge believed that "no enterprise can exist for itself alone. It ministers to some great need, it performs some great service, not for itself, but for others; or failing therein it ceases to be profitable and ceases to exist."

—*Failing Forward*

Put others ahead of you in your mind and heart today.

THE INSTRUMENT OF LEADERSHIP

John W. Gardner observed, "If I had to name a single all-purpose instrument of leadership, it would be communication." Perhaps you are familiar with my books on leadership; then you know that I believe everything rises and falls on leadership. What I haven't mentioned before is that leadership rises and falls on communication.

If you lead your team, give yourself these standards to live by as you communicate to your people:

1. Be consistent. Nothing frustrates team members more than leaders who can't make up their minds. One of the things that won the team over to Gordon Bethune when he was at Continental was the consistency of his communication. His employees always knew they could depend on him and what he said.

2. Be clear. Your team cannot execute if the members don't know what you want. Don't try to dazzle anyone with your intelligence; impress people with your straightforwardness.

3. Be courteous. Everyone deserves to be shown respect, no matter what the position or what kind of history you might have with him. By being courteous to your people, you set the tone for the entire organization.

Never forget that because you are the leader, your communication sets the tone for the interaction among your people. Teams always reflect their leaders. And never forget that good communication is never one-way. It should not be top-down or dictatorial. The best leaders listen, invite, and then encourage participation.

—*The 17 Indisputable Laws of Teamwork*

***Be aware today that your communication is setting
the tone with the people you lead.***

THE POWER OF A GROWTH
ENVIRONMENT

Just as the growth of tropical fish is limited by the size of the aquarium in which they live, you are affected by your environment. That's why it's crucial to create an environment of growth around you. That kind of place should look like this:

- *Others are ahead of you:* When you surround yourself with people from whom you can learn, you are more likely to grow.
- *You are still challenged:* Complacency kills growth.
- *Your focus is forward:* If you're thinking more about the past than the future, your growth has probably stopped.
- *The atmosphere is affirming:* Industrialist Charles Schwab said, "I have yet to find the man . . . who did not do better work and put forth greater effort under a spirit of approval than under a spirit of criticism."
- *You are out of your comfort zone:* Growth requires risk. Ronald E. Osborne stated, "Unless you do something beyond what you've already mastered, you will never grow."
- *Others are growing:* When it comes to growth, it's better to swim in a school than to try to do everything on your own.
- *There is a willingness to change:* Clayton G. Orcutt declared, "Change itself is not progress, but change is the price that we pay for progress."
- *Growth is modeled and expected:* In the best possible environment, growth is not only allowed, but leaders model it and expect it from everyone. And when that happens, everyone's potential is off the charts.

—*Your Road Map for Success*

**Take responsibility for creating an environment
of growth for your team members.**

THE HEART OF LEADERSHIP

Where is your heart when it comes to serving others? Do you desire to become a leader for the perks and benefits? Or are you motivated by a desire to help others?

If you really want to become the kind of leader that people want to follow, you will have to settle the issue of servanthood. If your attitude is to be served rather than to serve, you may be headed for trouble. If this is an issue in your life, then heed this advice:

- Stop lording over people, and start listening to them.
- Stop role-playing for advancement, and start risking for others' benefit.
- Stop seeking your own way, and start serving others.

It is true that those who would be great must be like the least and the servant of all.

Albert Schweitzer wisely stated, "I don't know what your destiny will be, but one thing I know: The ones among you who will be really happy are those who have sought and found how to serve." If you want to lead on the highest level, be willing to serve on the lowest.

—*The 21 Indispensable Qualities of a Leader*

Examine your motivation for leading others today.

INSTILL MOTIVATION

Vince Lombardi, the famed Green Bay Packers football coach, was a feared disciplinarian. But he was also a great motivator. One day he chewed out a player who had missed several blocking assignments. After practice, Lombardi stormed into the locker room and saw that the player was sitting at his locker, head down, dejected. Lombardi mussed his hair, patted him on the shoulder, and said, "One of these days, you're going to be the best guard in the NFL."

That player was Jerry Kramer, and Kramer says he carried that positive image of himself for the rest of his career. "Lombardi's encouragement had a tremendous impact on my whole life," Kramer said. He went on to become a member of the Green Bay Packers Hall of Fame and a member of the NFL's All-50-Year Team.

Everybody needs motivation from time to time. Never underestimate the power of it:

- Motivation helps people who know what they should do . . . to do it!
- Motivation helps people who know what commitment they should make . . . to make it!
- Motivation helps people who know what habit they should break . . . to break it!
- Motivation helps people who know what path they should take . . . to take it!

Motivation makes it possible to accomplish what you should accomplish.

—*25 Ways to Win with People*

Motivate someone in your circle of influence today.

NOTES

WEEK 17

EXPERIENCE IS NOT
THE BEST TEACHER

How often do you pause to reflect on your experiences?

How do you record what you've learned?

How do you evaluate your year?

BE SOLUTION ORIENTED

Most people can see problems. That doesn't require any special ability or talent. Someone who thinks in terms of solutions instead of just problems can be a difference maker. A team filled with people who possess that mind-set can really get things done.

Your personality type, upbringing, and personal history may affect how solution oriented you are naturally. However, anyone can become solution oriented. Consider these truths that all solution-seeking people recognize:

Problems are a matter of perspective. Obstacles, setbacks, and failures are simply parts of life. You can't avoid them. But that doesn't mean you have to allow them to become problems. The best thing you can do is to meet them with a solution-oriented mind-set. It's just a matter of attitude.

All problems are solvable. Some of the great problem solvers have been inventors. Charles Kettering explained, "When I was research head of General Motors and wanted a problem solved, I'd place a table outside the meeting room with a sign: 'Leave slide rules here.' If I didn't do that, I'd find someone reaching for his slide rule. Then he'd be on his feet saying, 'Boss, you can't do it.'" Kettering believed all problems were solvable, and he helped to cultivate that attitude in others. If you want to be solution oriented, then you must be willing to cultivate that attitude in yourself too.

Problems either stop us or stretch us. Problems either hurt you or help you. Depending on how you approach them, they'll stop you from succeeding or stretch you so that you not only overcome them but also become a better person in the process. The choice is yours.

—*The 17 Essential Qualities of a Team Player*

Do problems stop or stretch you?

LEADERS ARE INTUITIVE

Under excellent leadership a problem seldom reaches gigantic proportions, because it is recognized and fixed in its early stages. Great leaders usually recognize a problem in the following sequence:

1. They sense it before they see it (intuition).
2. They begin looking for it and ask questions (curiosity).
3. They gather data (processing).
4. They share their feelings and findings to a few trusted colleagues (communicating).
5. They define the problem (writing).
6. They check their resources (evaluating).
7. They make a decision (leading).

Great leaders are seldom blindsided. They realize that the punch that knocks them out is seldom the hard one—it's the one they didn't see coming. Therefore, they are always looking for signs and indicators that will give them insight into the problem ahead and their odds of fixing it. They treat problems like the potential trespasser of an Indiana farm who read this sign on a fence post: "If you cross this field, you better do it in 9.8 seconds. The bull can do it in 10 seconds."

—*Developing the Leader Within You*

Pay attention to your intuition, and follow up when something strikes you.

WHAT CAN I LEARN FROM
WHAT HAPPENED?

I enjoy reading the comic strip *Peanuts* by Charles Schulz. In one of my favorites, Charlie Brown is at the beach building a beautiful sand castle. As he stands back to admire his work, it is suddenly consumed by a huge wave. Looking at the smooth sand mound that had been his creation a moment before, he says, "There must be a lesson here, but I don't know what it is."

That's the way many people approach adversity. They are so consumed by the events that they become bewildered and miss the whole learning experience. But there is always a way to learn from failures and mistakes. Poet Lord Byron was right when he stated, "Adversity is the first path to truth."

It's difficult to give general guidelines about how to learn from mistakes because every situation is different. But if you maintain a teachable attitude as you approach the process and try to learn *anything* you can about what you could do differently, you will improve yourself. When a person has the right mind-set, every obstacle introduces him to himself.

—*Failing Forward*

*Carve out some time today to reflect on recent
mistakes you've made.*

WHEN TO MAKE DECISIONS

Many people make decisions when things aren't going well. They look for relief in the despair of the valley instead of waiting for the clarity that comes from being on the mountaintop. Why? Because it takes a lot of effort to get to the mountaintop. And when you're experiencing the darkness of the valley, it's always tempting to make changes that you hope will relieve the discomfort.

When you are on top of the proverbial mountain, that is the time to make decisions. Here's why:

• You can see your situation more clearly.
• You are moving to something, not just from something.
• You leave those around you in a better position.
• You decide using positive data, not negative.
• You are more likely to move from peak to peak instead of valley to valley.

On the other hand, when you're in the valley, the most important thing you can do is persevere. If you keep fighting, you're likely to get your second wind, just as distance runners do. And it's said that only when runners are exhausted enough to reach that place do they find out what they can truly accomplish. If you keep persevering while you are in the valley, not only will you likely make it to higher ground where you can make better decisions, but you will also have developed character, which will serve you well throughout life.

—*The Difference Maker*

***Use the clarity of mountaintop moments to
make major decisions.***

ACHIEVERS VERSUS AVERAGE

What makes achievers excel? Why do some people skyrocket while others plummet? You know what I'm talking about. You can call it luck, blessing, or the Midas touch—call it whatever you want. But the truth is that some people just seem to achieve incredible things in spite of tremendous difficulties: They finish in the top 5 percent in nationwide sales for their company after losing key accounts. They find ingenious ways to increase profits for their department in the face of budget cuts. They earn a graduate degree while raising two children as a single parent. They discover awesome business opportunities while colleagues don't see any at all. Or they recruit winner after winner into their organization despite what looks like an anemic labor pool. It doesn't matter what kind of work they do. Wherever they are, they just seem to make things happen.

Certainly all people like to think of themselves as above average. But achievers seem to leave "average" in the dust—so far behind them that ordinary seems a distant memory.

What makes the difference? Why do some people achieve so much? Is it . . . Family background? Wealth? Opportunity? High morals? The absence of hardship?

No, none of these things is the key. When it comes right down to it, I know of only one factor that separates those who consistently shine from those who don't: *the difference between average people and achieving people is their perception of and response to failure.* Nothing else has the same kind of impact on people's ability to achieve and to accomplish whatever their minds and hearts desire.

—*Failing Forward*

Accept failure as the price of success today
and keep striving forward.

NOTES

WEEK 18

~∾~

THE SECRET TO A GOOD MEETING IS THE MEETING BEFORE THE MEETING

Are your meetings structured?

Have you connected with the key influencer?

What is your plan for the next big change?

THE POWER OF COLLABORATION

Are you a collaborative person? You may not be working against the team, but that doesn't necessarily mean you're working for it. Do you bring cooperation and added value to your teammates—even to the people you don't enjoy being with?

To become a collaborative team player . . .

Think win-win-win. Usually when you collaborate with others, you win, they win, and the team wins. Find someone on the team with a similar role whom you have previously seen as a competitor. Figure out ways you can share information and work together to benefit both you and the team.

Complement others. Another way to collaborate is to get together with someone who has strengths in your area of weakness and vice versa. Seek out others on the team with complementary gifts and work together.

Take yourself out of the picture. Get in the habit of asking what's best for the team. For example, the next time you are at a problem-solving meeting and everyone is contributing ideas, instead of promoting yourself, ask yourself how the team would do if you were not involved in the solution. If it would do better, then propose ideas that promote and involve people other than yourself.

—The 17 Essential Qualities of a Team Player

**Be mindful to bring a spirit of collaboration and
cooperation into everything you do today.**

A CHECKLIST FOR CHANGE

Below are the questions you should review before attempting changes within an organization.

YES	NO	
____	____	Will this change benefit the followers?
____	____	Is this change compatible with the purpose of the organization?
____	____	Is this change specific and clear?
____	____	Are the top 20 percent (the influencers) in favor of this change?
____	____	Is it possible to test this change before making a total commitment to it?
____	____	Are physical, financial, and human resources available to make this change?
____	____	Is this change reversible?
____	____	Is this change the next obvious step?
____	____	Does this change have both short- and long-range benefits?
____	____	Is the leadership capable of bringing about this change?
____	____	Is the timing right?

The last question is the ultimate consideration for implementing change. Success in bringing about change will happen only if the timing is right.

—*Developing the Leader Within You*

Use this checklist to verify you're on track before your next meeting before the meeting.

EVERYONE CAN TEACH YOU SOMETHING

Have you ever met someone who felt compelled to play the expert all the time? Such people aren't much fun to be around after a while, because the only input they seem open to is their own. And as the saying goes, people won't go along with you unless they can get along with you.

If you really desire others to see you as an approachable person, go a step beyond just willingness to admit your weaknesses. Be willing to learn from them. One of the things I teach in *Winning with People* is the Learning Principle, which states, "Each person we meet has the potential to teach us something." I really believe that. If you embrace that idea, I believe you will discover two things. First, you will learn a lot, because every time you meet someone, it is a learning opportunity. Second, people will warm up to you. Complete strangers often treat me like an old friend, simply because I am open to them.

—*The 360° Leader*

Be open to what others can teach you today.

SHARE IDEAS

What is an idea worth? Every product begins with an idea. Every service begins with an idea. Every business, every book, every new invention begins with an idea. Ideas are what make the world move forward. So when you give people an idea, you give them a great gift.

One of the things I love about writing books is the process that it takes me through. It usually starts with a concept that I'm anxious to teach. I get a few ideas down on paper, and then I call together a group of good creative thinkers to help me test the concept, brainstorm ideas, and flesh out the outline. Every time we've done this, people have given me great ideas that I never would have come up with on my own. I have to say I'm very grateful.

One of the things I enjoy most about creative people is that they love ideas, and they always seem to have more coming. The more they give away, the more new ideas they seem to have. Creativity and generosity feed each other. That's one of the reasons I'm never reluctant to share ideas with others. I'm convinced that I will run out of time long before I run out of ideas. It's better to give some away and contribute to another person's success than to have them lying dormant in me.

—*25 Ways to Win with People*

*Let every meeting become a learning and
idea-sharing experience.*

BRING SOMETHING TO THE TABLE

For years I have used the expression "bring something to the table" to describe a person's ability to contribute to a conversation or to add value to others at a meeting. Not everyone does that. In life, some people always want to be the "guest." Wherever they go, they are there to be served, to have their needs met, to be the recipient. Because they possess that attitude, they never bring anything to the table for anyone else. After a while, that can really wear out the person who is always playing host.

As the leader of an organization, I am always looking for people who bring something to the table in the area of ideas. If they can be creative and generate ideas, that's great. But I also highly value people who are constructive, who take an idea that someone puts on the table and make it better. Often the difference between a good idea and a great idea is the value added to it during the collaborative thinking process.

If you always try to bring something of value to the table when you meet with your boss, you may be able to avoid a similar fate at work. If you don't, at the end of the day you just may get a note from the boss. Only yours will be a pink slip.

—*The 360° Leader*

When you meet with others, seek to add value to them.

NOTES

WEEK 19

~

BE A CONNECTOR, NOT JUST A CLIMBER

KEY GROWTH QUESTIONS FOR THE WEEK

What is your natural inclination?

How can you become a better connector?

How can you become a better climber?

THE LAW OF CONNECTION

The stronger the relationship you form with followers, the greater the connection you forge—and the more likely those followers will be to want to help you. Whether you're speaking in front of a large audience or chatting in the hallway with an individual, the guidelines are the same.

1. Connect with Yourself: You must know who you are and have confidence in yourself if you desire to connect with others.

2. Communicate with Openness and Sincerity: Legendary NFL coach Bill Walsh said, "Nothing is more effective than sincere, accurate praise, and nothing is more lame than a cookie-cutter compliment."

3. Know Your Audience: Learn people's names, find out about their histories, ask about their dreams. Speak to what *they* care about.

4. Live Your Message: Practice what you preach. That's where credibility comes from.

5. Go to Where They Are: I dislike any kind of barrier to communication. I adapt to others; I don't expect them to adapt to me.

6. Focus on Them, Not Yourself: The number one problem of inexperienced speakers and ineffective leaders is that they focus on themselves.

7. Believe in Them: It's one thing to communicate to people because you believe you have something of value to say. It's another to communicate with people because you believe they have value.

8. Offer Direction and Hope: French general Napoleon Bonaparte said, "Leaders are dealers in hope."

—*The 21 Irrefutable Laws of Leadership*

Intentionally connect with the people you lead today.

DON'T MISS OUT

People miss many opportunities for connection and the chance to build deeper relationships because they do not make themselves approachable. And notice that I am purposely using the phrase "make themselves." Approachability has little to do with other people's boldness or timidity. It has everything to do with how you conduct yourself and what messages you send to others.

Years ago I saw a piece called "The Art of Getting Along," which stated,

> Sooner or later, a man, if he is wise, discovers that life is a mixture of good days and bad, victory and defeat, give and take. He learns that it doesn't pay to be a too-sensitive soul, that he should let some things go over his head like water off a duck's back. He learns that he who loses his temper usually loses out, that all men have burnt toast for breakfast now and then, and that he shouldn't take the other fellow's grouch too seriously . . . He learns that most others are as ambitious as he is, that they have brains as good or better, that hard work, not cleverness, is the secret of success. He learns that no man ever gets to first base alone, and that it is only through cooperative effort that we move on to better things. He realizes (in short) that the "art of getting along" depends about 98 percent on his own behavior toward others.

If you want to make yourself agreeable and approachable to others, then you need to put them at ease.

—*Winning with People*

Are you making yourself approachable?

WALK SLOWLY THROUGH THE HALLS

One of the greatest mistakes leaders make is spending too much time in their offices and not enough time out among the people. Leaders are often agenda driven, task focused, and action oriented because they like to get things done. They hole up in their offices, rush to meetings, and ignore everyone they pass in the halls along the way. What a mistake! First and foremost, leadership is a people business. If you forget the people, you're undermining your leadership, and you run the risk of having it erode away. Then one day when you think you're leading, you'll turn around and discover that nobody is following and you're only taking a walk.

Relationship building is always the foundation of effective leadership. Leaders who ignore the relational aspect of leadership tend to rely on their position instead. Or they expect competence to do "all the talking" for them. True, good leaders are competent, but they are also intentionally connected to the people they lead.

One of the best ways to stay connected to your people and keep track of how they're doing is to approach the task informally as you move among the people. As you see people in the parking lot, chat with them. Go to meetings a few minutes early to see people, but don't start in on the agenda until you've had time to catch up. And, as the title of this section suggests, take time to walk slowly through the halls. Connect with people and give them an opportunity to make contact with you.

—*The 360° Leader*

**Slow down and connect with the people
you work with and lead.**

BUILD TRUST

I have learned that trust is the single most important factor in building personal and professional relationships. Warren Bennis and Burt Nanus call trust "the glue that binds followers and leaders together." Trust implies accountability, predictability, and reliability. More than anything else, followers want to believe in and trust their leaders. They want to be able to say, "Someday I want to be like him or her." People first must believe in you before they will follow your leadership.

Trust must be built day by day. It calls for consistency. Some of the ways a leader can betray trust include: breaking promises, gossiping, withholding information, and being two-faced. These actions destroy the environment of trust necessary for the growth of potential leaders. And when a leader breaks trust, he must work twice as hard to regain it.

People will not follow a leader they do not trust. It is the leader's responsibility to actively develop that trust in him from the people around him. Trust is built on many things:

Time. Take time to listen and give feedback on performance.
Respect. Give someone respect and he will return it with trust.
Unconditional Positive Regard. Show acceptance of the person.
Sensitivity. Anticipate feelings and needs of the potential leader.
Touch. Give encouragement—handshake, high five, pat on the back.

Once people trust their leader as a person, they become able to trust his leadership.

—*Developing the Leaders Around You*

Take responsibility for earning trust with your followers.

SLOW DOWN

Most people who want to lead are naturally fast. But if you want to become a better leader, you actually need to slow down. You can move faster alone. You can garner more individual honors alone. But to lead others, you need to slow down enough to connect with them, engage them, and take them with you.

If you have children, you instinctively understand this. The next time you need to get something done around the house, try doing it two ways. First, have your kids help. That means you need to enlist them. You need to train them. You need to direct them. You need to supervise them. You need to redirect them. You need to recapture and reenlist them when they wander off. It can be pretty exhausting, and even when the work is completed, it may not be to the standard you'd like.

Then try doing the task alone. How much faster can you go? How much better is the quality of the work? How much less aggravation is there to deal with?

Working alone is faster (at least in the beginning), but it doesn't have the same return. If you want your children to learn, grow, and reach their potential, you need to pay the price and take the time and trouble to lead them through the process. It's similar with employees. Leaders aren't necessarily the first to cross the finish line—people who run alone are the fastest. Leaders are the first to bring all of their people across the finish line. The payoff to leadership—at work or home—comes on the back end.

—*The 360° Leader*

Be willing to move at others' pace today.

NOTES

_____

_____

_____

_____

_____

_____

_____

_____

_____

_____

_____

_____

_____

_____

_____

_____

_____

_____

WEEK 20

❧

THE CHOICES YOU MAKE,
MAKE YOU

KEY GROWTH QUESTIONS FOR THE WEEK

What major choices have changed your life?

*What key choices have you made (or will you make)
to guide your leadership?*

Are you prepared to make difficult choices?

JUST PRACTICING

In *The 17 Indisputable Laws of Teamwork*, I wrote about pioneer aviator Charles Lindbergh, mentioning that even his solo flight across the Atlantic Ocean was really a team effort, since he had the backing of nine businessmen from St. Louis and the help of the Ryan Aeronautical Company, which built his plane. But that doesn't take away from his personal effort. For more than thirty-three hours, he flew alone and covered an incredible 3,600 miles.

That's not the kind of task a person just goes out and does. He has to work up to it. How did Lindbergh do that? A story from his friend Frank Samuels gives insight into the process. In the 1920s, Lindbergh used to fly mail out of St. Louis. Occasionally he would go out to San Diego to check on the progress of his plane, the *Spirit of Saint Louis*, which was being built there. Samuels sometimes went along with him, and the two men would stay overnight in a small hotel there. One night Samuels woke up shortly after midnight and noticed that Lindbergh was sitting by the window looking at the stars. It had been a long day, so Samuels asked, "Why are you sitting there at this hour?"

"Just practicing," answered Lindbergh.

"Practicing what?" asked Samuels.

"Staying awake all night."

When he could have been enjoying a well-deserved rest, Lindbergh was putting forth the effort to improve himself. It's an investment that paid off for him—and it can do the same thing for you.

—*The 17 Essential Qualities of a Team Player*

Are you currently making choices that will prepare you for future opportunities?

IT'S YOUR CHOICE

Poet, critic, and dictionary writer Samuel Johnson observed, "He who has so little knowledge of human nature as to seek happiness by changing anything but his own disposition will waste his life in fruitless efforts and multiply the grief which he purposes to remove." Most people want to change the world to improve their lives, but the world they need to change first is the one inside themselves. That is a choice—one that some are not willing to make.

The longer you live, the more your life is shaped by your choices. You decide what you will eat. (This is one of the most common ways small children begin to assert their independence.) You decide what toys to play with. You decide whether you will do your homework or watch TV. You choose which friends to spend time with. You choose whether to finish high school, whether you will go to college, who you will marry, what you will do for a living. The longer you live, the more choices you make—and the more responsible you are for how your life is turning out.

I don't know what kind of circumstances you've had to face in your life. You may have had a really tough time. You may have faced extreme hardship or suffered terrible tragedies. However, your choices are still your choice.

—*The 17 Essential Qualities of a Team Player*

Take complete responsibility for the choices you are making.

THE DESTINATION MYTH

If you want to succeed, you need to learn as much as you can about leadership before you have a leadership position. When I meet people in social settings and they ask me what I do for a living, some of them are intrigued when I say I write books and speak. And they often ask what I write about. When I say leadership, the response that makes me chuckle most goes something like this: "Oh. Well, when I become a leader, I'll read some of your books!" What I don't say (but want to) is: "If you'd read some of my books, maybe you'd become a leader."

Good leadership is learned in the trenches. Leading as well as they can wherever they are is what prepares leaders for more and greater responsibility. Becoming a good leader is a lifelong learning process. If you don't try out your leadership skills and decision-making process when the stakes are small and the risks are low, you're likely to get into trouble at higher levels when the cost of mistakes is high, the impact is far reaching, and the exposure is greater. Mistakes made on a small scale can be easily overcome. Mistakes made when you're at the top cost the organization greatly, and they damage a leader's credibility.

How do you become the person you desire to be? You start now to adopt the thinking, learn the skills, and develop the habits of the person you wish to be. It's a mistake to daydream about "one day when you'll be on top" instead of handling today so that it prepares you for tomorrow. As Hall of Fame basketball coach John Wooden said, "When opportunity comes, it's too late to prepare." If you want to be a successful leader, learn to lead before you have a leadership position.

—*The 360° Leader*

Try out a new leadership skill today.

GROWTH IS A CHOICE

Most people fight against change, especially when it affects them personally. As novelist Leo Tolstoy said, "Everyone thinks of changing the world, but no one thinks of changing himself." The ironic thing is that change is inevitable. Everybody has to deal with it. On the other hand, growth is optional. You can choose to grow or fight it. But know this: people unwilling to grow will *never* reach their potential.

In one of his books, my friend Howard Hendricks asks the question, "How have you changed . . . lately? In the last week, let's say? Or the last month? The last year? Can you be *very specific*?" He knows how people tend to get into a rut when it comes to growth and change. Growth is a choice, a decision that can really make a difference in a person's life.

Most people don't realize that successful and unsuccessful people do not differ substantially in their abilities. They vary in their desires to reach their potential. And nothing is more effective when it comes to reaching potential than commitment to personal growth.

—*Your Road Map for Success*

*In what specific ways have you changed lately
to reach your potential?*

THE POWER OF RIGHT CHOICES

Life is a matter of choices, and every choice you make makes you. What will you do for your career? Who will you marry? Where will you live? How much education will you get? What will you do with today? But one of the most important choices you will make is *who will you become!* Life is not merely a matter of holding and playing a good hand as you would hope to do in a card game. What you start with isn't up to you. *Talent* is God-given. Life is playing well the hand you have been dealt. That is determined by your choices.

The talent-plus people are the ones who maximize their talent, reach their potential, and fulfill their destiny.

I was reading a book by Dr. Seuss to my grandchildren called *Oh, the Places You'll Go!* In it, I found a wonderful truth. It said,

> You have brains in your head.
> You have feet in your shoes.
> You can steer yourself
> Any direction you choose.

I believe that with all my heart. My prayer is that you steer yourself in the right direction and make right choices that will empower you to become a talent-plus person, build upon the foundation of your abilities, and live your life to its fullest potential.

—*Talent Is Never Enough*

*Maximize your talent by steering your entire
life in the right direction.*

NOTES

WEEK 21

———— ❧ ————

INFLUENCE SHOULD BE LOANED BUT NEVER GIVEN

KEY GROWTH QUESTIONS FOR THE WEEK

Are there people you need to speak up for?

What do you expect in return for your influence?

Do you need to increase your level of influence with others?

LOOKING FOR INFLUENCE

Sociologists tell us that even the most introverted individual will influence ten thousand other people during his or her lifetime! This amazing statistic was shared with me by my associate Tim Elmore. Tim and I concluded that each one of us is both influencing and being influenced by others. That means that all of us are leading in some areas, while in other areas we are being led. No one is excluded from being a leader or a follower. Realizing your potential as a leader is your responsibility. In any given situation with any given group, there is a prominent influencer.

The prominent leader of any group is quite easily discovered. Just observe the people as they gather. If an issue is to be decided, who is the person whose opinion seems most valuable? Who is the one others watch the most when the issue is being discussed? Who is the one with whom people quickly agree? Most importantly, who is the one the others follow? Answers to these questions will help you discern who the real leader is in a particular group.

—*Developing the Leader Within You*

As you look for people to whom you will lend your influence, observe how much influence they already have.

WHEN YOU PARTNER WITH OTHERS

Thomas Jefferson observed, "A candle loses nothing when it lights another candle." That is the real nature of partnership. I find that many people don't think that way. They believe that sharing means losing something. But I don't think that's true.

Every person possesses one of two mind-sets: scarcity or abundance. People with a scarcity mind-set believe that there's only so much to go around, so you have to scrap for everything you can and protect whatever you have at all costs. People with an abundance mind-set believe there's always enough to go around. If you have an idea, share it; you can always come up with another one. If you have money, give some of it away; you can always make more. If you have only one piece of pie, let someone else eat it; you can bake another one.

I believe that in this area, you get from life what you expect. You can hoard what little you have and receive no more. Or you can give what you have, and you will be rewarded with abundance. Your attitude makes the difference. So if you partner with another person and give generously, one way or another you're going to get back more than you gave.

—*Winning with People*

Consider how your mind-set—of either scarcity or abundance—is impacting your leadership.

DO FOR OTHERS WHAT THEY CAN'T
DO FOR THEMSELVES

Ambassador and poet Henry Van Dyke observed, "There is a loftier ambition than merely to stand high in the world. It is to stoop down and lift mankind a little higher." What a great perspective! Doing for others what they can't do for themselves is really a matter of attitude. I believe that whatever I've been given is to be shared with others. And because I have an abundance mind-set, I never worry about running out myself. The more I give away, the more I seem to get to give away.

No matter how much or how little you think you have, you have the ability to do for others what they cannot do for themselves. Exactly how you do that will depend on your unique gifts, resources, and history.

Nearly twenty-five years ago, Professor C. Peter Wagner, who was then on the faculty of Fuller Seminary, invited me to speak to audiences of pastors around the country about leadership. He put me on a national stage for the first time and gave me credibility that I didn't possess on my own.

Few things are of greater value to a prepared person than an opportunity. Why? Because opportunities increase our potential. Demosthenes, the great orator of ancient Greece, said, "Small opportunities are often the beginning of great enterprises." An opportunity seized is often a source of success. Help people win by giving them opportunities, and you will win with them.

—*25 Ways to Win with People*

Provide others with small opportunities to succeed, and then acknowledge and reward their success.

FIVE-STEP PROCESS OF TRAINING

The best type of training takes advantage of the way people learn. I have found the best training method to be a five-step process:

Step 1: I model. The process begins with my doing the tasks while the person being trained watches. When I do this, I try to give the person an opportunity to see me go through the whole process. When people see the task performed correctly and completely, it gives them something to try to duplicate.

Step 2: I mentor. I continue to perform the task, but this time the person I'm training comes alongside me and assists in the process. I also take time to explain not only the *how* but also the *why* of each step.

Step 3: I monitor. The trainee performs the task and I assist and correct. It's especially important during this phase to be positive and encouraging. Work with him until he develops consistency. Once he's gotten down the process, ask him to explain it to you.

Step 4: I motivate. I take myself out of the task at this point and let the trainee go. My task is to make sure he knows how to do it without help and to keep encouraging him. At this time the trainee may want to make improvements to the process. Encourage him to do it, and at the same time learn from him.

Step 5: I multiply. This is my favorite part of the whole process. Once the new leaders do the job well, it becomes their turn to teach others how to do it. As teachers know, the best way to learn something is to teach it.

—*Developing the Leaders Around You*

*Begin your influence loan by developing a person
using the five-step training process.*

MAKE SOME INTRODUCTIONS

My dad, Melvin Maxwell, has done many incredible things for me during the course of my life. One of the things that impacted me most was his introducing me to great men. As a teenager, I met Norman Vincent Peale, E. Stanley Jones, and other exceptional men of the faith. And because I had declared my intention to go into the ministry, my father asked these preachers to pray for me. I can't express in words what that did for me.

Today, I am often in a position to do for others what my father did for me. I love introducing young people to my heroes. I love helping people make business contacts. There are often times when I meet someone, and as we talk, it just hits me: I need to introduce this person to so-and-so. That can mean walking somebody across the room, making a phone call on his or her behalf, or arranging a meeting. Several years ago, I was talking to Anne Beiler, the founder of Auntie Anne's, the pretzel company, and she mentioned in passing that Chick-fil-A's founder, Truett Cathy, was one of her heroes. Since I knew Truett, I offered to introduce them to each other. I hosted a dinner party for them at my house, and it was a great night.

Please don't get the impression that you have to know someone famous to help others in this area. Sometimes it's as simple as introducing one friend to another or one business associate to another. Just make connections. Be the bridge in people's relationships with others.

—*25 Ways to Win with People*

Create a relational bridge for someone today.

NOTES

WEEK 22

—❧—

FOR EVERYTHING YOU GAIN,
YOU GIVE UP SOMETHING

KEY GROWTH QUESTIONS FOR THE WEEK

What trades have you made?

What additional trades do you need to make?

What will you trade for the betterment of your people?

COMMIT TO PAY THE PRICE FOR CHANGE

American dramatist and screenwriter Sidney Howard remarked, "One half of knowing what you want is knowing what you must give up before you get it." Change always costs you something, if not monetarily, then in time, energy, and creativity. In fact, if change *doesn't* cost you anything, then it isn't real change!

As you consider how to make the changes needed to improve and grow, it is important to measure the cost of change compared to the cost of the status quo. You have to do your homework. That often makes the difference between:

Change = Growth
and
Change = Grief

What will the changes you desire really cost you?

Management expert Tom Peters gives a perspective on this. He suggests, "Don't rock the boat. Sink it and start over." If you desire to be creative and do something really innovative, that's sometimes what it takes. You must destroy the old to create something new. You cannot allow yourself to be paralyzed by the idea of change.

—*The Difference Maker*

Is what you want worth what you must give up to get it?

SIGNIFICANCE OVER SECURITY

Most people enjoy feeling secure. It's a natural desire, one that psychologist Abraham Maslow recognized as important in the hierarchy of human needs. But to keep moving to a higher level and reach your potential, you also have to be willing to bypass another landmark and trade security for significance.

Bob Buford talks about the landmark ability of shifting your attention to significance in his book *Halftime*. As he sees it, our lives naturally break into two halves, with a midpoint usually falling somewhere between ages thirty and fifty. He says, "The first half of life has to do with getting and gaining, learning and earning. . . . The second half is more risky because it has to do with living beyond the immediate." And he adds, "If you do not take responsibility for going into halftime and ordering your life so that your second half is better than the first, you will join the ranks of those who are coasting their way to retirement." According to Buford, the key to making your second half count is to make the shift to significance. The result is that you will experience a life of purpose and see the fulfillment of your life's mission.

No matter when you make the change to significance, whether it's during your "halftime" or at some other time of life, know that it is one of the most significant, life-changing steps—and landmarks—on the success journey. It's a decision that's always worth the price.

—*Your Road Map for Success*

Are you striving to make a difference, or have
you been tempted to coast?

PAY THE PRICE THAT ATTRACTS LEADERS

Success always comes at a price. That is a lesson I learned a long time ago. My father taught me that a person can pay now and play later, or he can play now and pay later. Either way, he is going to pay.

Creating a climate for potential leaders also requires a leader to pay a price. It begins with personal growth. The leader must examine himself, ask himself the hard questions, and then determine to do the right thing regardless of atmosphere or mood. There are few ideal and leisurely settings for the disciplines of growth. Most of the significant things done in the world were done by persons who were either too busy or too sick to do them. Emotion-based companies allow the atmosphere to determine the action. Character-based companies allow the action to determine the atmosphere.

Successful leaders recognize that personal growth and the development of leadership skills are lifetime pursuits. Warren Bennis and Burt Nanus, in *Leaders: The Strategies for Taking Charge*, did a study of ninety top leaders in all fields. They found that "it is the capacity to develop and improve their skills that distinguishes leaders from their followers." They came to the conclusion that "leaders are perpetual learners."

—*Developing the Leaders Around You*

Be willing to pay the price to be a perpetual learner.

GROWING TO YOUR POTENTIAL

Novelist H. G. Wells held that wealth, notoriety, place, and power are no measures of success whatsoever. The only true measure of success is the ratio between what we might have been and what we have become. In other words, success comes as the result of growing to our potential.

It's been said that our potential is God's gift to us, and what we do with it is our gift to Him. But at the same time, our potential is probably our greatest untapped resource. Henry Ford observed, "There is no man living who isn't capable of doing more than he thinks he can do."

We have nearly limitless potential, yet too few ever try to reach it. Why? The answer lies in this: we can do *anything*, but we can't do *everything*. Many people let everyone around them decide their agenda in life. As a result, they never really dedicate themselves to *their* purpose in life. They become a jack-of-all-trades, master of none—rather than a jack-of-few-trades, focused on one.

If that describes you more than you'd like, you're probably ready to take steps to make a change. There are four principles to put you on the road to growing toward your potential:

1. Concentrate on one main goal.
2. Concentrate on continual improvement.
3. Forget the past.
4. Focus on the future.

When you know your purpose in life and are growing to reach your maximum potential, you're well on your way to being a success.
—*Your Road Map for Success*

*What must you give up to focus on the one
thing that will set you apart?*

THE LAW OF SACRIFICE

If you desire to become the best leader you can be, then you need to be willing to make sacrifices in order to lead well. If that is your desire, then here are some things you need to know:

1. There Is No Success Without Sacrifice: Leaders must give up to go up. Talk to leaders, and you will find that they have made repeated sacrifices. Effective leaders sacrifice much that is good in order to dedicate themselves to what is best.

2. Leaders Are Often Asked to Give Up More than Others: The heart of leadership is putting others ahead of yourself. It's doing what is best for the team. For that reason, I believe that leaders have to give up their rights.

3. You Must Keep Giving Up to Stay Up: If leaders have to give up to go up, then they have to give up even more to stay up. What gets a team to the top isn't what keeps it there. The only way to stay up is to give up even more.

4. The Higher the Level of Leadership, the Greater the Sacrifice: The higher you go, the more it's going to cost you. And it doesn't matter what kind of leadership career you pick. You will have to make sacrifices. You will have to give up to go up.

—*The 21 Irrefutable Laws of Leadership*

Are you willing to give up to go up?

NOTES

WEEK 23

—⁓—

THOSE WHO START THE JOURNEY WITH YOU SELDOM FINISH WITH YOU

KEY GROWTH QUESTIONS FOR THE WEEK

What is your reaction to people's leaving the team?

Have you been waiting too long for people to go to the next level?

Where are the next key players coming from?

HIRE FOR SKILL AND EXPERIENCE

Back when I thought that attitude was everything, I tried to hire people with the best attitudes and figured I could get them up to speed in their skills. Now that I am older and more experienced, I realize that I had things backward. Now I hire primarily for skill and experience. Here's why: when it comes to talent and skill, a person can grow only a limited amount. On a scale from one to ten, most people can improve in a skill area only about two points. So, for example, if you are naturally a "6" as a leader, you may be able to grow to an "8" if you work at it. However, if you are a "2," you can work as hard as you want and you will never reach even average. The old saying of coaches is true: you can't get out what God didn't put in.

Attitude, however, is a different matter. There is no growth ceiling. Even a person with a "2" attitude can grow to become a "10." So even someone whose attitude isn't the best can turn that around.

On the day that I decided as a leader to hire only people with successful track records to key positions in my organization, my professional life changed. The entire team became more productive, and my organization began going to another level. That's not to say that I began hiring people with bad attitudes; I didn't. It wasn't an either/or decision. It was a both/and decision. Competence, experience, and positive attitude are a winning combination.

—*The Difference Maker*

How have you selected the people on your team?

MANAGING THE REVOLVING DOOR

If you lead your team, you are responsible for making sure the revolving door moves in such a way that the players who are joining the team are better than those who are leaving. One way you can facilitate that is to place high value on the good people already on the team.

Every team has three groups of players. The first is the starters, who directly add value to the organization or who directly influence its course. The second is the bench players, who indirectly add value to the organization or who support the starters. The third group is a core group within the starters that I call the inner-circle members. Without these people the team would fall apart. Your job is to make sure each group is continually developed so that bench players are able to step up to become starters, and starters are able to step up to become inner-circle members.

If you're not sure who the inner-circle members are on your team, then try this exercise: Write the names of the people on your team who are starters. Now determine the people you could most easily do without. One by one, check off the names of the people whose loss would hurt the team least if they left. At some point you will end up with a smaller group of people without whom the team would be dead. That's your inner circle. (You can even rank the remaining people in order of importance.)

It's a good exercise to remind you of the value of people on the team. And by the way, if your treatment of those people doesn't match their value, you run the risk of losing them and having your revolving door work against you.

—*The 17 Indisputable Laws of Teamwork*

***Does your treatment of your inner-circle members
match their value?***

LINK UP WITH OTHERS

Some people aren't very outgoing and simply don't think in terms of team building and team participation. As they face challenges, it never occurs to them to enlist others to achieve something.

As a people person, I find that hard to relate to. Whenever I face any kind of challenge, the very first thing I do is to think about the people I want on the team to help with it. I've been that way since I was a kid. I've always thought, *Why take the journey alone when you can invite others along with you?*

I understand that not everyone operates that way. But whether or not you are naturally inclined to be part of a team is really irrelevant. If you do everything alone and never partner with other people, you create huge barriers to your own potential. Dr. Allan Fromme quipped, "People have been known to achieve more as a result of working with others than against them." What an understatement! It takes a team to do anything of lasting value. Besides, even the most introverted person in the world can learn to enjoy the benefits of being on a team. (That's true even if someone isn't trying to accomplish something great.)

For the person trying to do everything alone, the game really is over. If you want to do something big, you must link up with others. One is too small a number to achieve greatness.

—*The 17 Indisputable Laws of Teamwork*

*As you face challenges, think about who you
can enlist to come alongside you.*

DEALING WITH THE WEAK LINK

If you're a team leader, you cannot ignore the issues created by a weak link. For the various kinds of teams, different solutions are appropriate. If the team is a family, then you don't simply "trade" weak people. You lovingly nurture them and try to help them grow, but you also try to minimize the damage they can cause to other family members. If the team is a business, then you have responsibilities to the owner or stockholders. If you've offered training without success, then a "trade" might be in order. If the team is a ministry and training has made no impact, then it might be appropriate to ask the weak people to sit on the sidelines for a while. Or they might need some time away from the team to work on emotional or spiritual issues.

No matter what kind of situation you face, remember that your responsibilities to people come in the following order: to the organization, to the team, and then to the individual. Your own interests—and comfort—come last.

—*The 17 Indisputable Laws of Teamwork*

*If you are the leader, it is your responsibility to address
the problem of a weak link on your team.*

KNOWING WHO TO DEVELOP

Often I am asked in leadership conferences, "How do you know which staff person to hire?" I always laugh and say, "You never know for sure," and my track record underscores that comment! However, here are some guidelines I have tried to follow when looking for staff:

- Know what you need before you start looking for someone.
- Take time to search the field.
- Call many references.
- Have several interviews.
- Include your associates in some interviews and ask for their input.
- Interview the candidates' spouses.
- Check out the candidates' track records.
- If possible, have a trial run to see if job and potential staff match.
- Ask hard questions, such as, "Why did you leave?"; "What can you contribute?"; "Are you willing to pay the price?"
- Trust your instincts.

If someone you're considering looks good on paper but makes you feel bad inside, go slowly. In fact, back off and let an associate take over the interviewing process; then compare conclusions. I only hire a person if it looks good *and* feels good.

—*Developing the Leader Within You*

Remember that you can lose with good players on your team, but you cannot win without them.

NOTES

WEEK 24

—— ❦ ——

FEW LEADERS ARE
SUCCESSFUL UNLESS A LOT OF
PEOPLE WANT THEM TO BE

KEY GROWTH QUESTIONS FOR THE WEEK

Who supports you?

How do you say thank you?

Who are your mentors?

SURROUND YOURSELF WITH LEADERS

Great leaders—the truly successful ones who are in the top 1 percent—all have one thing in common. They know that acquiring and keeping good people is the leader's most important task. An organization cannot increase its productivity—but people can! The asset that truly appreciates within an organization is people. Systems become dated. Buildings deteriorate. Machinery wears. But people can grow, develop, and become more effective if they have a leader who understands their potential value.

The bottom line is that you can't do it alone. If you really want to be a successful leader, you must develop other leaders around you. You must establish a team. You must find a way to get your vision seen, implemented, and contributed to by others.

Most leaders have followers around them. Few leaders surround themselves with other leaders. The ones who do bring great value to their organizations. And not only is their burden lightened, but their vision is carried on and enlarged. The key to surrounding yourself with other leaders is to find the best people you can, then develop them into the best leaders they can be. Great leaders produce other leaders.

—*Developing the Leaders Around You*

***You need other people to succeed; you need other leaders
to go to the highest level.***

THE LAW OF THE INNER CIRCLE

When we see any incredibly gifted person, it's always tempting to believe that talent alone made him successful. To think that is to buy in to a lie. Nobody does anything great alone. Leaders do not succeed alone. A leader's potential is determined by those closest to him. What makes the difference is the leader's inner circle.

To practice the Law of the Inner Circle, you must be intentional in your relationship building. As you consider whether individuals should be in your inner circle, ask yourself the following questions:

1. Do they have high influence with others?
2. Do they possess strengths in my areas of weakness?
3. Do they add value to me and my organization?
4. Do they positively impact other inner circle members?
   —*The 21 Irrefutable Laws of Leadership*

*Be highly intentional and strategic in
building your inner circle.*

LET PEOPLE KNOW YOU NEED THEM

The day that I realized I could no longer do everything myself was a major step in my development as a person and a leader. I've always had vision, plenty of ideas, and vast amounts of energy. But when the vision gets bigger than you, you really only have two choices: give up on the vision or get help. I chose the latter.

No matter how successful you are, no matter how important or accomplished, you *do* need people. That's why you need to let them know that you cannot win without them. President Woodrow Wilson said, "We should not only use all the brains we have—but all that we can borrow." Why stop with just their brains? Enlist people's hands and hearts too! Another president, Lyndon Johnson, was right when he said, "There are no problems we cannot solve together, and very few that we can solve by ourselves."

—*25 Ways to Win with People*

*Take time today to let the people around you know
how much you need and appreciate them.*

THE LAW OF DIVIDENDS

At this stage of my life, everything I do is a team effort. When I first started teaching seminars, I did everything. Certainly there were other people pitching in, but I was just as likely to pack and ship a box as I was to speak. Now, I show up and teach. My wonderful team takes care of everything else. Even the book you're reading was a team effort. My team is my joy. I would do anything for the people on my team because they do everything for me:

- My team makes me better than I am.
- My team multiplies my value to others.
- My team enables me to do what I do best.
- My team gives me more time.
- My team represents me where I cannot go.
- My team provides community for our enjoyment.
- My team fulfills the desires of my heart.

Building a team for the future is just like developing a financial nest egg. It may start slowly, but what you put in brings a high return—similar to the way that compound interest works with finances. Try it and you will find that the Law of Dividends really works. *Investing in the team compounds over time.*

—*The 17 Indisputable Laws of Teamwork*

Investing in your team pays dividends not only for them and the organization but also for you.

PEOPLE NEED TO KNOW THEY HELPED

Whenever someone tells me how valuable the people on my team are to him, I encourage him to tell the individuals who were so helpful. Why? Because people need to know that they helped someone.

"Good leaders make people feel that they're at the very heart of things, not at the periphery," says author and leadership expert Warren Bennis. "Everyone feels that he or she makes a difference to the success of the organization. When that happens people feel centered and that gives their work meaning." Walter Shipley of Citibank says, "We have 68,000 employees. With a company this size, I'm not 'running the business.' . . . My job is to create the environment that enables people to leverage each other beyond their own individual capabilities. . . . I get credit for providing the leadership that got us there. But our people did it." Shipley understands what successful leaders know: people need to know that they made an important contribution to reaching the goal.

It's not a sign of weakness to let others know you value them. It's a sign of security and strength. When you're honest about your need for help, specific with others about the value they add, and inclusive of others as you build a team to do something bigger than you are, everybody wins.

—*25 Ways to Win with People*

Tell the members of your team why *they are valuable to you.*

NOTES

WEEK 25

YOU ONLY GET ANSWERS TO THE QUESTIONS YOU ASK

KEY GROWTH QUESTIONS FOR THE WEEK

Is your ego getting in the way of your growth?

What questions do you need to ask yourself?

Who can you ask other questions?

ASK WHY, NOT WHO

The next time you experience a failure, think about why you failed instead of *who* was at fault. Try to look at it objectively so that you can do better next time. My friend Bobb Biehl suggests a list of questions to help you analyze any failure:

- What lessons have I learned?
- Am I grateful for this experience?
- How can I turn the failure into success?
- Practically speaking, where do I go from here?
- Who else has failed in this way before, and how can that person help me?
- How can my experience help others someday to keep from failing?
- Did I fail because of another person, because of my situation, or because of myself?
- Did I actually fail, or did I fall short of an unrealistically high standard?
- Where did I succeed as well as fail?

People who blame others for their failures never overcome them. They move from problem to problem, and as a result, they never experience success. To reach your potential, you must continually improve yourself, and you can't do that if you don't take responsibility for your actions and learn from your mistakes.

—Your Road Map for Success

Be the first to take responsibility for finding answers
when things go wrong for your team.

LEADERSHIP DEVELOPS DAILY, NOT IN A DAY

Becoming a leader is a lot like investing successfully in the stock market. If your hope is to make a fortune in a day, you're not going to be successful. What matters most is what you do day by day over the long haul. If you continually invest in your leadership development, letting your "assets" compound, the inevitable result is growth over time.

• *Phase 1:* I Don't Know What I Don't Know: As long as a person doesn't know what he doesn't know, he isn't going to grow.

• *Phase 2:* I Know That I Need to Know: Many people find themselves placed in a leadership position only to look around and discover that no one is following them. When that happens, we realize that we need to learn how to lead.

• *Phase 3:* I Know What I Don't Know: To grow as a leader I have to realize I don't have all the answers or the skills as a leader. I need others on my journey of growth.

• *Phase 4:* I Know and Grow, and It Starts to Show: When you recognize your lack of skill and begin the daily discipline of personal growth, exciting things start to happen.

• *Phase 5:* I Simply Go Because of What I Know: Your ability to lead becomes almost automatic. You develop great instincts. And that's when the payoff is incredible.

—*The 21 Irrefutable Laws of Leadership*

*Ask yourself (and honestly answer!) where you
are in the leadership process.*

CHOOSE A LEADERSHIP MODEL

Give careful thought to which leaders you will follow, because they will determine your course. I have developed six questions to ask myself before picking a model to follow:

Does my model's life deserve a following? This question relates to quality of character. I will become like the people I follow, and I don't want models with flawed character.

Does my model's life have a following? This question looks at credibility. If the person has no following, he or she may not be worth following.

What is the main strength that influences others to follow my model? What does the model have to offer me? What is his best? Also note that strong leaders have weaknesses as well as strengths. I don't want to inadvertently emulate the weaknesses.

Does my model produce other leaders? The answer to this question will tell me whether the model's leadership priorities match mine in regard to developing new leaders.

Is my model's strength reproducible in my life? If I can't reproduce his strength in my life, his modeling will not benefit me. But don't be too quick to say that a strength is not reproducible. Most are.

If my model's strength is reproducible in my life, what steps must I take to develop and demonstrate that strength? If you only answer the questions and never implement a plan to develop those strengths in yourself, you are only performing an intellectual exercise.

—*Developing the Leaders Around You*

Before enlisting a mentor, make sure you ask the right questions.

BELIEF DETERMINES EXPECTATION

If you want your talent to be lifted to its highest level, then you don't begin by focusing on your talent. You begin by harnessing the power of your mind. Your beliefs control everything you do. Accomplishment is more than a matter of working harder or smarter. It's also a matter of believing positively. Someone called it the "sure enough" syndrome. If you expect to fail, sure enough, you will. If you expect to succeed, sure enough, you will. You will become on the outside what you believe on the inside.

Personal breakthroughs begin with a change in your beliefs. Why? Because your beliefs determine your expectations, and your expectations determine your actions. A belief is a habit of mind in which confidence becomes a conviction that we embrace. In the long run, a belief is more than an idea that a person possesses. It is an idea that possesses a person. You need to expect to succeed. Does that mean you always will? No. You will fail. You will make mistakes. But if you expect to win, you maximize your talent, and you keep trying.

Attorney Kerry Randall said, "Contrary to popular opinion, life does not get better by chance, life gets better by change. And this change always takes place inside; it is the change of thought that creates the better life." Improvement comes from change, but change requires confidence. For that reason, you need to make confidence in yourself a priority. President Franklin Delano Roosevelt asserted, "The only limit to our realization of tomorrow will be our doubts of today." Don't let your doubts cause your expector to expire.

—*Talent Is Never Enough*

How are your beliefs impacting your expectations?

DO THE RIGHT THING

Doing the right thing doesn't come naturally to any of us. As America's first president, George Washington, said, "Few men have virtue enough to withstand the highest bidder." Yet that is what we must do to develop the kind of character that will sustain us.

It's not easy to do the right thing when the wrong thing is expedient. Molière commented, "Men are alike in their promises. It is only in their deeds that they differ. The difference in their deeds is simple: People of character do what is right regardless of the situation."

One way that I've tried to control my natural bent to do wrong is to ask myself some questions (adapted from questions written by business ethicist Dr. Laura Nash):

1. Am I hiding something?
2. Am I hurting anyone?
3. How does it look from the other person's point of view?
4. Have I discussed this face-to-face?
5. What would I tell my child to do?

If you do the right thing—and keep doing it—even if it doesn't help you move ahead with your talent in the short term, it will protect you and serve you well in the long term. Character builds— and it builds you. Or as Dr. Dale Bronner, a board member of my nonprofit organization EQUIP, puts it, "Honesty is not something you do; honesty is who you are."

—*Talent Is Never Enough*

Determine to do the right thing—even when it hurts.

NOTES

WEEK 26

❧

PEOPLE WILL SUMMARIZE YOUR LIFE IN ONE SENTENCE— PICK IT NOW

KEY GROWTH QUESTIONS FOR THE WEEK

How important has a legacy been to you?

What do you want your legacy to be?

Are you living that legacy today?

THE LAW OF SIGNIFICANCE

It's safe to say that we all admire achievers. And we Americans especially love pioneers and bold individualists—people who fight alone, despite the odds or opposition: the settler who carves a place for himself in the wilds of the frontier, the old-west sheriff who resolutely faces an enemy in a gunfight, the pilot who bravely flies solo across the Atlantic Ocean, or the great scientist who changes the world through the power of his mind.

As much as we admire solo achievement, the truth is that no lone individual has done anything of value. The belief that one person can do something great is a myth.

Nothing of significance was ever achieved by an individual acting alone.

A Chinese proverb states that "behind an able man there are always other able men." The truth is that teamwork is at the heart of great achievement. The question isn't whether teams have value. The question is whether we acknowledge that fact and become better team players. That's why I assert that **one is too small a number to achieve greatness.** That is the Law of Significance.

You cannot do anything of *real* value alone. It may be a cliché, but it is nonetheless true: individuals play the game, but teams win championships.

—*The 17 Indisputable Laws of Teamwork*

Is a team helping you to achieve your dreams?

HOW TO RAISE UP LEADERS
WHO REPRODUCE LEADERS

In an article published by the *Harvard Business Review*, author Joseph Bailey examined what it took to be a successful executive. In conducting his research, he interviewed more than thirty top executives and found that every one of them learned firsthand from a mentor. If you want to raise up leaders who reproduce other leaders, you need to mentor them.

We've been told that in hospital emergency rooms, nurses have a saying: "Watch one, do one, teach one." It refers to the need to learn a technique quickly, jump right in and do it with a patient, and then turn around and pass it on to another nurse. The mentoring process for developing leaders works in a similar way. It happens when you take potential leaders under your wing, develop them, empower them, share with them how to become persons of influence, and then release them to go out and raise up other leaders. Every time you do that, you plant seeds for greater success. And as novelist Robert Louis Stevenson advised, "Don't judge each day by the harvest you reap but by the seeds you plant."

— *Becoming a Person of Influence*

Develop leaders who will develop other
leaders, not just followers.

ACHIEVEMENT OVER AFFIRMATION

Affirmation from others is fickle and fleeting. If you want to make an impact during your lifetime, you have to trade the praise you could receive from others for the things of value that you can accomplish. You can't be "one of the boys" and follow your destiny at the same time.

A friend once explained something to me that illustrates this concept very well. He grew up near the Atlantic Ocean, where people catch blue crabs for dinner. He told me that as they catch the crabs, they'll toss them into a bucket or basket. He said that if you have only one crab in the basket, you need a lid to keep it from crawling out, but if you've got two or more, you don't. That didn't make any sense to me until he explained further. He said that when there are several crabs, they will drag each another down so that none of them can get away.

I've found that some unsuccessful people act the same way. They do all kinds of things to keep others from getting ahead, trying to prevent them from improving themselves or their situation. They use all kinds of devices to keep others in the basket with them: playing politics, promoting mediocrity, role-playing, and so on. But the good news is that if people try to do that, you don't have to buy into their belief system. You can stay out of the basket by refusing to be a crab. You may have to face opposition and live through times of insecurity, but you'll also experience freedom, increased potential, and satisfaction. Raise yourself up, and raise others with you.

—*Your Road Map for Success*

*Take the high road and speak well of others,
no matter what they say about you.*

DEVELOP AND FOLLOW YOUR PRIORITIES

There's an old saying that if you chase two rabbits, both will escape. Unfortunately that is what many people seem to do. They don't focus their attention, and as a result, they become ineffective. Perhaps the reason is that people in our culture have too many choices—nearly unlimited options. Management expert Peter Drucker recognized this phenomenon. He said, "Concentration is the key to economic results. No other principle of effectiveness is violated as constantly today as the basic principle of concentration. . . . Our motto seems to be, 'Let's do a little bit of everything.'"

If you want to develop your talent, you need to focus. If you're going to focus, you need to work on knowing what your true priorities are and then following them. This is something I have learned to do over time. I love options. I like to have the freedom to pursue the best course of action at any given moment. When I was in my twenties, I spent a lot of time doing things that had little return. In my thirties, I did better, but I still wasn't as focused as I should have been. It wasn't until I reached forty that I started to become highly selective about where I spent my time and energy. Today I filter just about everything I do through my top priority: *Am I adding value to people?* For me, it all comes down to that.

—*Talent Is Never Enough*

Are you remaining focused on your top priority?

THE LAW OF LEGACY

I believe that every person leaves some kind of legacy. For some it's positive. For others it's negative. But here's what I know: we have a choice about what legacy we will leave, and we must work and be intentional to leave the legacy we want.

Know the legacy you want to leave. Most people simply accept their lives—they don't lead them. I believe that people need to be proactive about how they live, and I believe that is especially true for leaders. Someday people will summarize your life in a single sentence. My advice: pick it now!

Live the legacy you want to leave. I believe that to have any credibility as a leader, you must live what you say you believe. If you want to create a legacy, you need to live it first. You must become what you desire to see in others.

Choose who will carry on your legacy. I don't know what you want to accomplish in life, but I can tell you this: a legacy lives on in people, not things. Too often leaders put their energy into organizations, buildings, systems, or other lifeless objects. But only people live on after we are gone. Everything else is temporary.

Make sure you pass the baton. Just about anybody can make an organization look good for a moment, but the best leaders lead today with tomorrow in mind. They make sure they invest in leaders who will carry their legacy forward. Why? Because a leader's lasting value is measured by succession.

—*The 21 Irrefutable Laws of Leadership*

Spend time reflecting on the lasting investments you would like to make and creating a plan to achieve them.

NOTES

Books by Dr. John C. Maxwell
Can Teach You How to Be A REAL Success

Relationships

Encouragement Changes Everything
25 Ways to Win With People
Winning With People
Relationships 101
The Treasure of a Friend
The Power of Partnership in the Church
Becoming a Person of Influence
Be A People Person
The Power of Influence
Ethics 101

Attitude

The Difference Maker
The Journey From Success to Significance
Attitude 101
Failing Forward
Your Bridge to a Better Future
Living at the Next Level
The Winning Attitude
Be All You Can Be
The Power of Thinking Big
Think on These Things
The Power of Attitude
Thinking for a Change

Equipping

Talent is Never Enough
Equipping 101
Developing the Leaders Around You
The 17 Essential Qualities of a Team Player
Success One Day at a Time
The 17 Indisputable Laws of Teamwork
Your Road Map for Success
Today Matters
Partners in Prayer

Leadership

Leadership Gold
Go for Gold
*The 21 Most Powerful Minutes
in a Leader's Day*
Revised & Updated 10th Anniversary
Edition of *The 21 Irrefutable
Laws of Leadership*
The 360 Degree Leader
Leadership Promises for Every Day
Leadership 101
The Right to Lead
The 21 Indispensable Qualities of a Leader
Developing the Leader Within You
The Power of Leadership

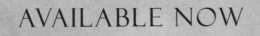